GOD'S CREATION
OF THE SEXUAL UNION

Complete list of Christian books by Gary Schulz

The Greatest Command
Hope for the Depressed
Become a Biblical Marriage Counselor
May They Be One
Relationships —Why Jesus Came
From God's Perspective
From Victim to Victory
The Discipling Father
Setting the Captives Free
New Wine New Wineskins
God's Creation of the Sexual Union
If You Love Me...
Partners
Saved from our Enemies
Good News of Jesus Christ
Eternal Life What Is It?
God's Creation of Work
The Power Of God's Grace
God's Creation, The Family
Marriage Enrichment
Passing Your Faith
Freedom From Anger
Clearly Seen
Creation to Rebellion to Restoration
Oil In Your Lamp
Wimps!
Controlling Parent Controlling Child
Restoring Broken Walls

GOD'S CREATION
OF THE SEXUAL UNION

A Biblical Study

Gary Schulz

Contents

Chapter One

God's Creation Under Attack

When God created the universe, the earth and all living creatures, he created it all as very good in his sight. At the end of each day, God looked at what he created and he proclaimed that what he saw was good. (Genesis 1:4, 10, 12, 18, 21, 25) After he completed his creation, he looked it over and proclaimed it to be "very good".

> God saw all that he had made, and it was very good. And there was evening, and there was morning—the sixth day. Genesis 1:31(NIV)

We cannot improve upon God's creation. It was created perfectly good and magnificently beautiful. However, there was one aspect of his creation that God said was not good.

> The LORD God said, "It is not good for the man to be alone. I will make a helper suitable for him." Genesis 2:18(NIV)

God finished his creation by creating a woman for man so that he would not be alone. Man was created out of the elements of the earth, but woman was created out of the elements of the man. Something was removed from the man, and God made the woman out of what was removed.

> But for Adam no suitable helper was found. So the LORD God caused the man to fall into a deep sleep; and while he was sleeping, he took one of the man's ribs and closed up the place with flesh. Then the LORD God made a woman from the rib he had taken out of the man, and he brought her to the man.
>
> The man said, "This is now bone of my bones and flesh of my flesh; she shall be called 'woman,' for she was taken out of man."
>
> For this reason a man will leave his father and mother and be united to his wife, and they will become one flesh.
>
> The man and his wife were both naked, and they felt no shame. Genesis 2:20-25(NIV)

It is as though Adam was incomplete after God removed the part of him for creating the woman. Then he reunited them as one to complete the man again. This is certainly a mystery, but it is obvious from these verses that God created man and woman by creating woman out of the man. Then he created marriage as the means for them to be one again.

God created both man and woman and also commanded them to have children and multiply and to rule over his creation through their offspring.

> So God created man in his own image, in the image of God he created him; male and female he created them.
>
> God blessed them and said to them, "Be fruitful and increase in number; fill the earth and subdue it. Rule over the fish of the sea and the birds of the air and over every living creature that moves on the ground." Genesis 1:27-28(NIV)

The sexual union between man and woman is part of God's creation. It consummates the marriage covenant of being one, and it is also the means by which God creates new human beings. What a beautiful union. God creates new people out of the loving union between a man and woman. In this union and in this new birth is another part of his creation, the family. All was good and perfect as God created it.

All of God's creation is perfect, good and beautiful as God originally created it. But even though we cannot improve upon it, we can pervert, distort and corrupt it. Not only can man defame his creation, the devil is intent upon robbing it of all beauty, harmony and life. What was once so good and beautiful has been strewn with filth. The devil and man have intently taken the sexual union, created by God, and have replaced its beauty with disgusting perversions. The once beautiful union has all but lost its majestic purpose as given by God. We have rejected God by our behavior. Man has been robbed of God's intended purpose through his creation of the sexual union that was to be reserved just for marriage. He has lost the delightful prosperity that proceeds from living as God purposed for it. All of mankind suffers as a consequence of man's perversions.

The statistics clearly reveal how man has lost what was created so magnificently beautiful.

- The divorce rate is one divorce for every two marriages.
- 39.7% of all births are to unmarried women. *(National Center for Health Statistics. 2007)*
- Over 12 million unmarried partners live together in 6,008,007 households. *(U.S. Census Bureau. "American Community Survey: 2005-2007)*
- The number of cohabiting unmarried partners increased by 88% between 1990 and 2007. *(U.S. Census Bureau. "America's Families and Living Arrangements: 2007.")*
- Homosexuality is being pushed as an accepted normal union. Homosexuals are even proclaiming themselves as married with the rights of having children. (Obviously they cannot have their own.)

- Most adults today have participated in premarital sex. Women (15-44 years of age): 84.9% Men (20-44 years of age): 91.3% *(Fertility, Family Planning, and Reproductive Health of U.S. Women: Data From the 2002 National Survey of Family Growth)* (*Fertility, Contraception, and Fatherhood: Data on Men and Women From Cycle 6 (2002) of the National Survey of Family Growth)*
- Adultery: It is estimated that roughly 30 to 60% of all married individuals (in the United States) will engage in infidelity at some point during their marriage. *(Susceptibility to Infidelity in the First Year of Marriage, David M. Buss and Todd K. Shackelford, The University of Texas at Austin)*
- 1 out of every 6 American women has been the victim of an attempted or completed rape in her lifetime. 17.7 million American women have been victims of attempted or completed rape. *(National Institute of Justice & Centers for Disease Control & Prevention. Prevalence, Incidence and Consequences of Violence Against Women Survey. 1998.)*
- 1 child in every 58 suffers from parental abuse and neglect. 11% of the maltreatment is sexual abuse. *(Fourth National Incidence Study of Child Abuse and Neglect (NIS–4))*
- Pornography has become an epidemic and a ten to fourteen billion dollar industry.

It seems like everything in the world today incorporates sex. Most TV shows and movies expose sex and nudity, even when it is unnecessary to support the storyline. Advertisements are filled with sexual arousals. It doesn't seem to matter what the product, sex is used to draw attention. We have filled our legal obligations with politically correctness, using terms like, sexist, gay rights, gay pride, feminist, and diversity. Our sexual views are at the center of this battle of what is true and what is legally acceptable. There is a purposeful drive to make sexual perversions a legal moral issue if anyone were to oppose them. We have to be very careful what we say or practice in public regarding God's view on any moral issue.

Yet those who promote deviant sexual practices are fully protected and promoted.

What has happened to this beautiful union between a man and a woman? How can we repent and recover its perfect beauty? First, we must realize and believe that marriage and the sexual union are creations of God, and that God designed them to be lived out in a limited prescribed manner. We must seek out God's word to rediscover his original intent and his deeper purposes. Then we must submit to God and live according to his original design. We must obey God and live.

Further study: Sodom and Gomorrah Genesis 18:20-21, 19:1-26, 30-38.
What was the "grievous sin"? Why was it so difficult to leave the city? Why did Lot's wife look back? How did the environment affect Lot's daughters? Who were the Moabites and the Ammonites?

Reflection questions

What are your beliefs about sex?

How did you come to believe what you believe? What is your source of truth?

How has the culture or your personal circumstances formed your beliefs about sex?

Have your experiences been fulfilling? How have they blessed your life? How have they been a curse or detriment?

Have you been sexually abused? Are you a child of a broken or dysfunctional home? Were your parents married?

Chapter Two

The Creation of Man and Woman

We have already seen that man and woman and the sexual union were created by God and were seen as good in the eyes of God. Let's examine this creation in more detail to form a solid biblical foundation for our beliefs

Man Created in the Image of God

Man is like no other creature that God created; he was created in the image of God. Other animals may have similar sexual organs and means of reproduction, but these animals were not created in the image of God.

> Then God said, "**Let us make man in our image, in our likeness**, and let them rule over the fish of the sea and the birds of the air, over the livestock, over all the earth, and over all the creatures that move along the ground." So **God created man in his own image, in the image of God he created him; male and female he created them.** Genesis 1:26-27(NIV)

Man is obviously a physical being, but he is also a spiritual being. Man's sexual nature is far more spiritual than it is physical. This is because God is a spirit, and we were created in his image—like him. The sexual union between all other creatures may have similarities, but man's is uniquely different. Similarities include a union between male and female, the reproductive process, and hormonal instincts or drives. This, for the most part, describes the similarities, but the human sexual experience goes far beyond merely having intercourse. We are the only creatures created in the image of God. God is spirit, and the sexual union has a spiritual component that far outweighs our physically biological component.

God is spirit, and his worshipers must worship in spirit and in truth. John 4:24(NIV)

When animals die, they are gone. But man is a spiritual being. When he dies, his spirit lives on. On the last day there will be a resurrection of the dead, and our bodies will be changed from physical bodies to spiritual bodies. (1 Corinthians 15:42-44).

This is all very mysterious, and no man fully understands this transformation. But what we all need to realize is that we are much more than physical beings. We are foremost created to be spiritual beings. Sex may be a physical act, but for man, it is much, much more spiritual than it is physical. This aspect is what separates our sexual union from all of the animals of God's creation.

When animals are in heat they go "crazy" because they are driven by their hormones. We do not expect animals to restrain themselves. That is how God made them. They will have sex in public, without shame and with any partner that is willing. Animals have sex as they are driven to have sex. They are not expected to be under self-control, and they do not sin in their sexual acts.

Man is driven by his hormones as well. But there is great shame if he does not control his physical drives. Many sins are the result of uncontrolled and improper sexual behavior. Why is that? It is because he was not created like all the other physical beings. He was created in the image of God, and his sexual acts are filled with spiritual meaning, purpose and consequences. Unfortunately, most of us are oblivious to the spiritual side of sex and the responsibilities placed upon our behavior.

Also, when we are relationally abused, which includes sexual abuse, we find that our spiritual being becomes wounded and scarred. We are very spiritually vulnerable, and our own sexual union(s) may be adversely affected by the abuse that was perpetrated upon us. If we were not spiritual beings, created in the image of God, we would not be vulnerable to sexual abuse.

Man Created from the Dust of the Ground

We read that Adam and all other creatures were created from the dust of the ground.

> **...the LORD God formed the man from the dust of the ground and breathed into his nostrils the breath of life, and the man became a living being**. Genesis 2:7(NIV)

> **Now the LORD God had formed out of the ground all the beasts of the field and all the birds of the air**. Genesis 2:19(NIV)

Clearly, man's physical body is nothing more than the elements of the earth. Most of our body is water. We eat fruits, grains and vegetables that grow in the earth, and from them we nourish our bodies and grow. When we die, our flesh decomposes back into simple organic matter.

But notice that God "breathed into his nostrils the breath of life, and man became a living being". Man is much more than a physical being, made up of the elements of the earth. He is a spiritual being made alive by the breath or Spirit of God. All other animals are biologically alive, but only man has received the breath of life from the Spirit of God.

Woman Created from Man

How was Eve, the first woman, created? Unlike Adam, she was not created directly from the elements of the earth. The first woman was created from a portion of Adam.

> But for Adam no suitable helper was found. So the LORD God caused the man to fall into a deep sleep; and while he was sleeping, **he took one of the man's ribs and closed up the place with flesh. Then the LORD God made a woman from the rib he had taken out of the man**, and he brought her to the man.
>
> The man said, "**This is now bone of my bones and flesh of my flesh; she shall be called 'woman,' for she was taken out of man.**"
> Genesis 2:20-23(NIV)

God removed a part of the man and made a woman from this portion. Adam was now missing a part of himself. But he could look across and see the woman, and see the missing part in beautiful living form. As Adam said, "This is now bone of my bones and flesh of my flesh; she shall be called 'woman,' for she was taken out of man."

Obviously, a woman is physically different from man. Her sexual parts are different, and her beauty is different. In fact, a woman is described as beautiful, but a man is described as handsome. Her features are soft and delicate; a man's is hard, rugged and hairy. A woman is mostly smaller and weaker.

The sexual differences go far beyond the physical. A woman's feelings tend to be tender and emotionally sensitive. Women tend to be much more verbal, and they have a need to talk through and from their feelings, whereas men tend talk through their logical thoughts with much fewer words. Women tend to nurture their children and cultivate a warm environment in the home. The spiritual differences between men and women are numerous. It does not require too much observation and insight to witness that men and women are very different biologically and spiritually.

And just as Adam lost a part of his original creation when man removed a part of him to create the woman, man today strives to complete his existence by being united with a wife. Because of sin, marriage can be a very painful trial, but most men and women desire and seek to be happily married.

Nakedness and the Sexual Union

Today we equate nakedness with shame. We all have private parts that are covered up so that no one can see them except ourselves in privacy. The animals do not have private parts, and they do not have a covering of clothing over any parts of their bodies. Only men and women cover up certain parts of their bodies so they cannot be seen. But it was not always that way. Before man sinned, man and woman were totally naked and they felt no shame or embarrassment. They were not even aware that they were naked because there was nothing to hide. When sin entered into their lives, so did shame. Because of their disobedience, they hid their nakedness from each other and they hid themselves from God. Obedience to God's way of living was their life-giving relationship with God and with each other. Disobedience planted the roots of severed relationships— between man and woman and between man and God. All mankind has suffered these lost relationships ever since. We have found the need to hide our naked selves from one another and from God out of the fear of our distrust in others and our own personal shame.

When the woman saw that the fruit of the tree was good for food and pleasing to the eye, and also desirable for gaining wisdom, she took some and ate it. She also gave some to her husband, who was with her, and he ate it. **Then the eyes of both of them were opened,**

and they realized they were naked; so they sewed fig leaves together and made coverings for themselves.

Then the man and his wife heard the sound of the LORD God as he was walking in the garden in the cool of the day, and they hid from the LORD God among the trees of the garden. But the LORD God called to the man, "Where are you?"

He answered, "I heard you in the garden, and **I was afraid because I was naked; so I hid**."

And he said, "**Who told you that you were naked?** Have you eaten from the tree that I commanded you not to eat from?"
Genesis 3:6-11(NIV)

This account is both physical and spiritual. Why do we need to cover up certain parts of our bodies? These parts are just skin with various shapes like any other part of our bodies. Why do we feel the need to cover up our sexual parts? What is the big deal? The answer is found by looking beyond the physical and coming to understand what goes on sexually in our hearts and spirits. Remember, we are both physical and spiritual beings. The sexual identity and sexual acts are obviously physical, but they are much more deeply spiritual in nature. Not so for other animals; and we see that they are totally unaware of any nakedness.

Our sexual union is tied very closely to our spiritual unity with other people. Man was created like God to be loved and to love. The sexual union is intimately tied to this basic character of God and man. Sex without relationship is just biological, just an animal function. For man, the sexual union is designed by God to be a relational union first and a biological union to follow the spiritual union.

There are many types of relationships among man, but marriage is the very closest. In marriage we can be totally physically naked before our partner without embarrassment or shame. This was God's intent. Marriage is also the place where we can become spiritually naked before our spouse. When there is trust and love, we can express our thoughts, our emotions, our struggles, our ambitions, our dreams, our passions, our shortcomings and motives. Marriage is an opportunity to walk together as one with another person, and this unity is only as compete as the degree to which we are open and trusting to one another emotionally, spiritually and mentally. This is the essence of the nakedness that Adam and Eve experienced before they disobeyed.

The true depth of life from the sexual union comes from this trusted, spiritual nakedness and love. Without this committed union of love, the sexual union is robbed of its spiritual unity and becomes only a hormonal, biological release.

What is Sin?

All sin is relational. Sin is an offense against man, ourselves or God. We can sin directly against God, but all sin against another man, woman, child or ourselves is also against God, since man was created for God's purposes. God's greatest commands are to love God and to love one another. (Matthew 22:37-40) Sin is opposite to love. Man was not aware of his nakedness—his need to cover his sexual parts—until he sinned. What happened?

First let's discuss love. Love and sin are opposites. The world has perverted the understanding of love. It has made love to be a self-serving behavior. We use phases like, "I love my new car" or "I love summer." The focus is on how something favorably affects us. But that is not a biblical understanding of love. If God is love, and if we have been created in the image of God, then we need to know God's love, not the world's perversion of love.

Love is our decisive attitudes and actions toward others by keeping their welfare at a higher regard than our own welfare. There are many verses on love, but let's consider just a few.

Greater love has no one than this, that he lay down his life for his friends. John 15:13(NIV)

Love is patient, love is kind. It does not envy, it does not boast, it is not proud. It is not rude, it is not self-seeking, it is not easily angered, it keeps no record of wrongs. Love does not delight in evil but rejoices with the truth. It always protects, always trusts, always hopes, always perseveres. 1 Corinthians 13:4-7

We were created in the image of God, so our original nature was to be like God in love. This is how we unite with God, and it is also how we unite with each other.

And so we know and rely on the love God has for us. **God is love. Whoever lives in love lives in God, and God in him.** 1 John 4:16(NIV)

When man sinned, his focus changed from love to self. Before sin, man had nothing to hide, for every thought and every action was directed toward the welfare of others. If someone could look into his heart and thoughts, all they would see is love for others. But once sin entered man, his heart and thoughts became self-centered and evil. Now he had much to hide out of embarrassment and shame.

He also became very vulnerable to other sinners. Before sin he could trust everyone else with his heart and thoughts because they had his best interest in mind. But now, with sin, we all walk around without complete trust. The only one we can trust with our welfare is ourselves. With sin, we have become a very isolated society of every man for himself. And so has our need to hide ourselves from others. We can no longer walk around naked, allowing others to see the private parts of our bodies, nor the private parts of our thoughts and hearts.

The sexual union between a man and woman is a private opportunity for a husband and wife to appear naked before each other. In a true marriage they are naked so that both can see each other's sexual parts. And because we are also spiritual beings, in a marriage, we allow each other to see what truly goes on inside our hearts and thoughts. We become naked in body, soul, thoughts and spirit before each other. In order for this to happen completely, we must love each other completely.

Reflection questions

What defines a man? What defines a woman?

Have you ever thought about why we cannot tickle ourselves? What is ticklishness?

How private are you with your thoughts and feelings? How is it different with your spouse?

Why do we hide certain bodily parts? Why do we hide some of our thoughts and feelings?

What drives you to sexual pleasure? Hormones? Excitement? Love and unity?

Is your sexual behavior confined to your marriage relationship?

Chapter Three

Basic Differences Between Men and Women

We might think that the differences between the sexes are obvious, but males and females are much more diverse than we first recognize. Certainly there are similarities, and there should be since Eve was created out of Adam. But there are also many differences because part of Adam was missing to create Eve, and became Eve's makeup.

Physical Differences

Obviously, men and women have different sexual organs. No one denies that. But let's look one step further.

We describe women as beautiful, pretty, cute, gorgeous, etc. A man would be offended to be described with one of these attributes; yet women are flattered.

Men are described as big and strong and handsome. They are ruddy, rugged and hairy, whereas women are soft, smooth and delicate.

Men in general are larger and stronger than women, and women are to be protected by men and treated as physically weaker.

Husbands, in the same way be considerate as you live with your wives, and **treat them with respect as the weaker partner** and as heirs with you of the gracious gift of life, so that nothing will hinder your prayers.
1 Peter 3:7(NIV)

Women by nature wear their hair longer than men.

Does not the **very nature of things** teach you that if a man has long hair, it is a disgrace to him, but that if a woman has long hair, it is her glory? For long hair is given to her as a covering.
1 Corinthians 11:14-15(NIV)

Women dress differently than men. They wear dresses to enhance their femininity, where as men would be embarrassed to try one on, even in the privacy of their own room. Women wear all kinds of fancy jewelry and frilly edges. Men wear baseball caps and sweatshirts. Men wear clothes that portray their work—work boots, hardhats, leather gloves, etc. Women wear clothes that identify them as housewives and moms.

A woman must not wear men's clothing, nor a man wear women's clothing, for the LORD your God detests anyone who does this.
Deuteronomy 22:5(NIV)

Obviously, our culture is degrading the differences between men and women. Mostly, women are dressing more like men and taking on men's roles. I believe a woman can wear jeans and a sweatshirt and still appear very much a woman. However, she is not nearly as feminine looking as when she wears a dress and all the other adornments that only women wear.

Communication

Clearly there are similarities. But just as clearly, there are major differences. Men tend to be analytical thinkers and talkers. They think in cause and effect. They are problem solvers, and when they talk, they are trying to fix something that is wrong, achieve a goal, go somewhere, or make something happen. Women, on the other hand, have many more words than men. They can talk logically as men, but they have another mode of communication that comes from their hearts. They talk to express their feelings without trying to logically solve their feelings. Somehow their problems are resolved just by expressing themselves and having a feeling listener. After their heartfelt expressions, their problem seems resolved; although for the man, the problem has not been fixed without something that has to be changed or accomplished.

Pink and Blue

Emerson Eggerichs has a ministry called *Love and Respect*, modeled after Ephesians 5:33. In his seminars and book by that title, he says that men have blue hearing aids and women have pink ones. The man sees things from his male viewpoint, and the woman sees things from her female viewpoint.

There are two books written by the Feldhahns, *For Men Only* and *For Women Only*. Each of these books is based on extensive studies of the needs of men and women, respectively. It becomes very obvious that man is not created like woman and woman is not created like man. We are beautifully different, but we must seek out the beautiful differences and walk in them. If we do not, we find divorce, hurt, wounds, perversions, inverted identities and ultimately a loss of spiritual life in ourselves, our families and society.

Man's Identity to His Work

Man was created to work. Work is not his curse; his work was created for him before he ever sinned against God.

> The LORD God took the man and put him in the Garden of Eden to work it and take care of it. Genesis 2:15(NIV)

The hardship and toil in his work is the curse, not the work itself. His work was made toilsome because he listened to his wife and ate of the tree that God forbid him to eat.

> To Adam he said, "**Because you listened to your wife** and ate from the tree about which I commanded you, 'You must not eat of it,' "Cursed is the ground because of you; through painful toil you will eat of it all the days of your life. It will produce thorns and thistles for you, and you will eat the plants of the field. By the sweat of your brow you will eat your food until you return to the ground, since from it you were taken; for dust you are and to dust you will return." Genesis 3:17-19(NIV)

God has made man responsible for obeying his commands and for taking care of his creation. That is his work. He created woman to be his helper. She is not his slave to do his work for him. She is his soul partner. She may labor too, but her labor is different. She, obviously, is given the task of bearing and nurturing children. She was created with the biological abilities and the nurturing abilities that man does not have. Together they raise up children for the next generation of leaders who are to care for and rule over God's creation, but their roles are different and not interchangeable. We may try, but the result is not fruitful. There has never been a woman who could impregnate another woman. Neither has there been a man who bore a child or fed the child from his breasts. Those are the obvious differences that are indisputable. But there are other differences that are disputed today.

Man was created to work. He was created with an inner drive to find male identity in his work. Women work too, and they may be very good at what they do, but men look to work for their masculine identity. They look to work for their purpose for living. They are driven to produce, to create, to fight, to provide—they are men.

Women have a beautiful place in man's work. The woman is not man's subservient slave. She is his partner. Together they are a beautiful team. Without him, she is incomplete. Without her, he is incomplete. They have a common purpose in life as ordained by God—if they seek him for their purpose. If they rebel and are disobedient, as Adam and Eve were, then this beautiful union will not exist and it will not be fruitful. Eve chose to rule over Adam. Adam chose to listen to his wife. They both lost and they both incurred upon themselves a curse from God. God knows what he is doing and what he has done. He created a beautiful partnership when he created man and woman. But man did not live up to his role, and woman did not submit to her role. And the harmony and beauty and fruitfulness was corrupted and nearly destroyed. It continues to be under attack today. It is our job to seek out the original design and walk in it.

Far too many men are finding their identity in the woman's role. And far too many women are finding identity in the man's role. This perversion is found in the workplace, the family, our government, the church, and society in general. It is taking its toll on the design and beauty of the sexual union. Women may make great workers and great leaders, but where are the men today? God created man first. God gave Adam the command not to eat of the tree in the middle of the garden, not Eve. She was not even created yet when the command was given to Adam. God held Adam accountable for listening to his wife, and not being obedient to what he heard directly from God. It is time for men to listen to God and walk in obedience to his instructions and to be diligent in his work. We are to call out to God,

May the favor *(beauty)* of the Lord our God rest upon us; establish the work of our hands for us—yes, establish the work of our hands. Psalm 90:17(NIV) (Italics added as an NIV alternate translation.)

Reflection questions

What was your father like? What did you like about him most? Least?

What was your mother like? What did you like about her most? Least?

As a man, have you ever found your purpose in life and in God by your work?

As a woman, how do you value the role as a wife? As a mother?

Chapter Four

The Creation of Marriage

Marriage is commonly referred to as an institution. I think of institutions as creations of man. Marriage is not a creation of man; it is a creation of God. If it were a creation of man, then man would have the power and authority to redefine it at any time. In fact, it would be possible and permissible for there to be more than one definition of marriage such that we would have a choice as to how to live out a marriage. There is a political issue today over just this issue. The debate is over the definition of marriage. Is it between a man and woman exclusively, or can it also include a man being married to a man, or a woman being married to a woman?

God defines marriage as between a man and a woman, exclusively. If we all believed in God and his determinations, then there would be no argument. The Bible is very clear. In fact, all major religions today are very clear on this issue. The issue comes down to the basic question, is marriage a creation of God or a creation (institution) of man? In other words, can man redefine marriage just by passing a law that gives legal identity, rights and acceptance to an alternative definition? The debate over the definition of marriage as being one man and one woman versus between two men or two women is really a religious debate. Is marriage a creation of God or not?

God created the sexual union to be experienced in marriage, and marriage only. The sexual union is part of marriage. God has created this union as the means for new life. New human beings are conceived in this union, and as a result, children are born into the family of the husband and wife. However, not only have we redefined marriage without God's consent, we have redefined the sexual union to meet our own desires. The practice of having sex outside of marriage is commonplace and commonly practiced by most unmarried adults. Cohabitation is common, multiple sex partners is common and 42% of our children are born outside of a marriage.

Homosexuality is just one more step in the direction of perverting God's original intent for marriage and the sexual union. Many churches now have accepted homosexuality and homosexual marriages. They have even condoned homosexuals as becoming pastors and spiritual leaders. They have ignored what the Bible says so that they can redefine marriage to fit their own agenda and desires. We are being told by government and religious leaders that we are not loving and accepting if we judge someone for his deviant sexual relationship. But the real perversion is one of truth. There are definite issues of right and wrong, and this issue is just as definite. In order to restore the sexual union to its original design, purpose and intent as defined by God, we must believe that it is not man's discretion to redefine marriage. We must seek what is right in God's eyes in all of life if we truly expect to have his life. *Jesus came to deliver us from sin, not to condone it.* We have the power of God living within us to live according to God's ways of living. Because of Jesus, there is now no excuse to continue in any deviant lifestyle.

Everyone who sins breaks the law; in fact, sin is lawlessness. But you know that he appeared so that he might **take away our sins**. And in him is no sin. **No one who lives in him keeps on sinning. No one who continues to sin has either seen him or known him.**

Dear children, **do not let anyone lead you astray**. **He who does what is right is righteous, just as he is righteous**. He who does what is sinful is of the devil, because the devil has been sinning from the beginning. The reason the Son of God appeared was to destroy the devil's work. **No one who is born of God will continue to sin, because God's seed remains in him; he cannot go on sinning, because he has been born of God**. This is how we know who the children of God are and who the children of the devil are: **Anyone who does not do what is right is not a child of God**; nor is anyone who does not love his brother. 1 John 3:4-10(NIV)

If we are to have God's sexual union restored to its original state, we must repent of our old ways and begin to live in God's ways. There are no other options!

Reunion Between Man and Woman

Remember that when God created woman that he created her out of a part of Adam. Now, the completion of Adam is Eve. The completion of man is woman. The two make a complete man. Marriage is the union of the two parts. Woman came out of man, and in marriage the two become one.

The Pharisees challenged Jesus about marriage and divorce. Responding to them, Jesus quoted the words that God spoke right after creating Eve (Genesis 2:24).

Some Pharisees came to him to test him. They asked, "Is it lawful for a man to divorce his wife for any and every reason?"

"Haven't you read," he replied, "that at the beginning **the Creator 'made them male and female,'** and said, 'For this reason a man will leave his father and mother and be united to his wife, and **the two will become one flesh'** ? So **they are no longer two, but one. Therefore**

23

what God has joined together, let man not separate." Matthew 19:3-6(NIV)

God created Adam. Then he separated a part of Adam from him to create Eve. Male and female are creations of God. This should be obvious to all. Then he united man and woman back together in a union of marriage. This reunion between man and woman, to make them one, is the creation of marriage. Man does not marry, God does. A pastor, priest or a legal representative does not perform a marriage. They may officiate over the ceremony. They may be a legal witness. But the uniting of man and woman is a mysterious act of God. Only God created man. Only God created woman. And only God created marriage. And as Jesus taught, only God can join or separate. "Let man not separate." Marriage belongs to God, not man.

Spiritual Union Based on Love, Not Sex

There is both a physical oneness and a spiritual oneness. Marriage is based on love for our marriage partner. If sex is the only thing holding the marriage together, there is only a selfish bodily union. But *if love is uniting them, then the sexual act transforms from a selfish hormonal fulfillment to love from both sides and mutual satisfaction. It is a transformation from a selfish pursuit without true unity to a beautiful union that lasts beyond the bedroom.*

Listen to Paul's instruction about how a man should love his wife.

Husbands, love your wives, as Christ loved the church and gave himself up for her, that he might sanctify her, having cleansed her by the washing of water with the word, so that he might present the church to himself in splendor, without spot or wrinkle or any such thing, that she might be holy and without blemish. In the same way **husbands should love their wives as their own bodies. He who loves**

his wife loves himself. For no one ever hated his own flesh, but nourishes and cherishes it, just as Christ does the church, because we are members of his body. "Therefore a man shall leave his father and mother and hold fast to his wife, and the two shall become one flesh." This mystery is profound, and I am saying that it refers to Christ and the church. However, let each one of you love his wife as himself, and let the wife see that she respects her husband. Ephesians 5:25-33(ESV)

Paul makes several comparisons in this passage of Scripture. He begins by stating that our love for our wives should be sacrificial for her welfare, not our own. It should be just as Jesus Christ gave up his life for his bride, the Church—meaning all of us. Then he says that we should love our wives as our own bodies, for whoever loves his wife love himself. This may sound like a strange statement unless we consider that woman was created out of man's body, and marriage is a reunion of her to man. Therefore we should love our wives as we love ourselves. Finally, he makes a comparison of the earthly marriage between husband and wife to the marriage between Christ and the Church. In other words, marriage has been given to us to represent and portray our eternal marriage with our Lord Jesus. Is it any wonder why marriage is under such intense attack by the devil and his world system? He wants to destroy the true meaning of our earthly union so that we will miss the union of Jesus with his people.

Remember that we are Jesus' body. We are also referred to as his bride. We are members of Christ through a marriage with Jesus. Those who have received his Spirit are one with him. Our bodies are meant for the Lord because we are all part of his body. Sexual sins are a sin directly against the body of Christ.

The body is not meant for sexual immorality, but for the Lord, and the Lord for the body. By his power God raised the Lord from the dead, and he will raise us also. **Do you not know that your bodies are members of Christ himself? Shall I then take the members of Christ**

and unite them with a prostitute? Never! Do you not know that **he who unites himself with a prostitute is one with her in body**? For it is said, "The two will become one flesh." But **he who unites himself with the Lord is one with him in spirit.**

Flee from sexual immorality. All other sins a man commits are outside his body, but **he who sins sexually sins against his own body. Do you not know that your body is a temple of the Holy Spirit, who is in you, whom you have received from God? You are not your own; you were bought at a price. Therefore honor God with your body.** 1 Corinthians 6:13-20(NIV)

What does it mean that we are the temple of the Holy Spirit? It is a marvelous thing, but God has sent his very own Spirit to live within us. It is by his Spirit that he takes us as his own. We were bought at the price of the blood of Jesus. We do not belong to ourselves; we belong to God. We have an obligation to use our bodies for the Lord's purposes. Sex with our wives is a good thing in God's eyes, but sex with anyone else is uniting Christ's body in a sinful union with someone else.

Marriage is the closest relationship that God created among men. This is the only relationship where the two unite as one. Actually, a marriage also includes God. It is God who makes us one. A Christian marriage includes the husband, his wife and Jesus. The Spirit of Christ is present in our sexual relationship with our wives. In fact, he fills our union with love and beauty, and he enjoys the union along with our enjoyment. That is why adultery and sexual immorality are so sinfully repulsive. As Paul wrote (above), "Shall I then take the members of Christ and unite them with a prostitute?" When a Christian man or woman has sex outside of marriage, Jesus is being subjected to the unholy union. And we fall under his judgment for doing so.

Marriage should be honored by all, and the marriage bed kept pure, for God will judge the adulterer and all the sexually immoral. Hebrews 13:4(NIV)

God Creates New People Out of the Union of Marriage

Obviously, new people are created when a man and woman unite together in a sexual act. There is no other means for the formation of new people. However, this can happen even if the man and woman are not married. Children can come out of rape, adultery, fornication (sex between unmarried) or marriage. It is God's intent for his creation to have children only through marriage. The sexual union is reserved for true marriage for the sake of upholding the intended spiritual beauty of marriage, and for the sake of raising up children in a marriage and family.

Marriage and family make the place that God designed for raising children to be God-fearing so that they would grow up to worship God with their lives and produce more God-fearing children. God hates divorce because divorce corrupts this anointed process for making new people to live and rule upon this earth. Look at God's very words to his people about marriage.

Another thing you do: You flood the LORD'S altar with tears. You weep and wail because he no longer pays attention to your offerings or accepts them with pleasure from your hands. You ask, "Why?" It is because the LORD is acting as the witness between you and the wife of your youth, because you have broken faith with her, though she is your partner, the wife of your **marriage covenant**.

Has not the LORD made them one? In flesh and spirit they are his. And why one? **Because he was seeking godly offspring**. So guard yourself in your spirit, and do not break faith with the wife of your youth.

"**I hate divorce**," says the LORD God of Israel, "and I hate a man's covering himself with violence as well as with his garment," says the LORD Almighty.

So guard yourself in your spirit, and **do not break faith**. Malachi 2:13-16

Notice that he calls it a marriage covenant. A contract can be broken if one side does not abide to their end of the contract. But a covenant is binding forever. It is not contingent upon your partner to uphold their commitment to love you. It is contingent upon your commitment to love your spouse. Most of our marriage vows finish with, "until death do us part". And we vow to stick together whether rich or poor, sick or healthy.

God also comes against a marriage where the two live together, but not in love. He says he hates divorce, but he also hates "a man's covering himself with violence". Violence could be physical, verbal, emotional, abandonment—any outright act of selfish offensive behavior. Children can be born out of a sexual union in marriage, but there also needs to be a spiritual union where love dominates.

When children are born into a true marriage they are covered with the security of this marriage relationship. Divorce and/or violence are not only devastating for the husband and wife; they are devastating to the children. These children will carry the scars into their adult lives and into their future families. God knew what he was doing when he created sex and marriage. If we want to prosper individually and as a society, we need to follow his design for marriage and family. Divorce, violence and children born out-of-wedlock is a recipe for disaster to all of mankind.

Further study: God is beautiful. Psalms 27:4. The devil was once a beautiful angel. Ezekiel 28:12&17, Isaiah 14:12-14 The devil distorts the beauty of God's creation with his own perverted beauty. How has sex been transformed with a distorted beauty?

Reflection questions

What was the marriage relationship like with your parents?

If you have been married, what was/is your marriage like?

How has your family relationships with your father and mother affected you in your relationships?

Up till now, how have you perceived the purpose for sex? What have been your viewpoints on sex outside of marriage? And, how have you perverted God's original intent for the sexual union with your practices?

Chapter Five

Our Bodies Belong to God

God created everything that exists. Everything that we see and everything that is beyond sight has been created by God. So, who owns everything? The answer should be obvious; everything belongs to the Creator, to God. But is that how we view creation? If I focus just on myself; what belongs to me? I might look at the things I own, the things that I purchased with my money and believe that they are mine. I worked hard in order to buy my house, my cars, my clothing and all of my possessions. Do they not belong to me?

There seems to be a dichotomy. Obviously, if God created everything, then everything belongs to him. But what about the things that I worked for, don't they belong to me? Jesus addresses this question in a parable.

"Suppose one of you had a servant plowing or looking after the sheep. Would he say to the servant when he comes in from the field, 'Come along now and sit down to eat'? Would he not rather say, 'Prepare my supper, get yourself ready and wait on me while I eat and drink; after that you may eat and drink'? Would he thank the servant because he did what he was told to do? So you also, when you have done everything you were told to do, should say, '**We are unworthy servants; we have only done our duty.**'" Luke 17:7-10(NIV)

First, all that we have comes from God. Even our work comes from God.

> You may say to yourself, "My power and the strength of my hands have produced this wealth for me." But remember the LORD your God, for it is he who gives you the ability to produce wealth, and so confirms his covenant, which he swore to your forefathers, as it is today. Deuteronomy 8:17-18(NIV)

We would have nothing if it were not for God who pours out his blessings upon us. We may take for granted what we have, but we should look to God daily and thank him for all that we possess. It all belongs to him, but he has poured out his abundant blessings upon us because he loves his creation, and especially man.

So, as the parable states, "We are unworthy servants". Our first obligation is to serve our creator with all that he has given to us. Then we can serve ourselves as God provides. Everything that we claim to own is on loan to us from God. He can take it back whenever he wants. And anytime that he commands us to serve him with his resources that he has put in our possession, we should serve him first. We are his servants who are enjoying the use of his possessions. But anytime that he demands, we are to use what he has given to us for his purposes.

Here are more difficult questions: Who do I belong to? Who owns my body? Who owns my mind and thoughts? Who owns my heart? Do I belong to myself?

Jesus was asked about the most important law of God.

> He answered: "'Love the Lord your God with **all your heart** and with **all your soul** and with **all your strength** and with **all your mind**'; and, 'Love your neighbor as yourself.'" Luke 10:27(NIV)

We are to love God with our entire being, including "all" of our heart, soul, strength and mind. Everything that we have is to be used to love God in service to him. That is our first obligation. After that, we can serve ourselves. Even our physical bodies do not belong to us alone. They first belong to God for his purposes. We have already reviewed Ephesians 5:25-33. In this passage Paul compares our bodies to the body of Jesus. We may have our own individual bodies, but if we take a bigger view of all Christians, we belong to Jesus as we make up his body.

> After all, no one ever hated his own body, but he feeds and cares for it, just as **Christ does the church**—for **we are members of his body**. Ephesians 5:29-30(NIV)

Sexual immorality is the practice of using the body that Jesus has given to us for purposes that do not honor God. Sexual immorality is sin for both the Christian and the non-Christian, for both degrade God's creation. But the Christian has been given the Spirit of God to live within him. When he uses his body in immoral acts, he is dragging the body of Christ into immorality. He not only sins against himself; he sins against the body of Christ.

> **Flee from sexual immorality**. All other sins a man commits are outside his body, but he who sins sexually sins against his own body. Do you not know that **your body is a temple of the Holy Spirit, who is in you**, whom you have received from God? **You are not your own; you were bought at a price. Therefore honor God with your body.** 1 Corinthians 6:18-20(NIV)

God created marriage. Our marriages belong to God. Marriage is the one and only acceptable place to have a sexual relation. In marriage, he united us with our spouse in such a way that our bodies belong to one another. This is not our design, but God's. He created man and woman and marriage.

> The husband should fulfill his marital duty to his wife, and likewise the wife to her husband. **The wife's body does not belong to her alone but also to her husband. In the same way, the husband's body does not belong to him alone but also to his wife.** Do not deprive each other except by mutual consent and for a time, so that you may devote yourselves to prayer. Then come together again so that Satan will not tempt you because of your lack of self-control.
> 1 Corinthians 7:3-5(NIV)

We use phrases like, "sexual freedom" or "free sex". We do not realize that when we intentionally live our lives to our own glory, rather than the glory of God, and when we see our lives as belonging to ourselves alone and when we begin to think that what we have is from ourselves; then we have planted the seeds of a curse from God. God will give us over to our perversions that have perverted God's glory and honor. In the end, our perversions will stand against us and destroy us.

> **For although they knew God, they neither glorified him as God nor gave thanks to him, but their thinking became futile and their foolish hearts were darkened.** Although they claimed to be wise, they became fools and exchanged the glory of the immortal God for images made to look like mortal man and birds and animals and reptiles.
> **Therefore God gave them over in the sinful desires of their hearts to sexual impurity for the degrading of their bodies with one another.** They exchanged the truth of God for a lie, and worshiped and served created things rather than the Creator—who is forever praised. Amen.
> Because of this, **God gave them over to shameful lusts**. Even their women exchanged natural relations for unnatural ones. In the same way the men also abandoned natural relations with women and were

inflamed with lust for one another. Men committed indecent acts with other men, and received in themselves the due penalty for their perversion.

Furthermore, since they did not think it worthwhile to retain the knowledge of God, **he gave them over to a depraved mind, to do what ought not to be done.** Romans 1:21-28(NIV)

In conclusion, all that we have belongs to God, and especially our bodies, our marriages and our sexual acts. They all belong to God for his glory, honor and purposes. Sexual immorality violates God's ownership of us.

Further study: "Struggle against sin" Hebrews 12:4 Paul beat his body. 1 Corinthians 9:24-27 How is our struggle against sin a sign of repentance (consider the following verses)?

"Enter by the narrow gate. For the gate is **wide** and the way is **easy** that leads to destruction, and those who enter by it are many. For the gate is **narrow** and the way is **hard** that leads to life, and those who find it are few. Matthew 7:13-14 (ESV)

Reflection questions

How do you honor God with your body?

How do you sin against God with your body?

How do you care for your body? How do you keep yourself healthy?

How do you use your body to serve and honor God?

Chapter Six

Sexual Sins

What is sin? First, let's realize that sin is relational. We sin against someone. It may be God, ourselves or someone else. For example, we steal from someone. We murder someone. We take the Lord's name in vain. We commit adultery with someone who is not our spouse, or someone who is someone else's spouse. We covet another man's possessions. We must come to realize that sin is not just wrong, it is wrong because it is harmful to others, ourselves and the community as a whole. Sin is deathly.

> When tempted, no one should say, "God is tempting me." For God cannot be tempted by evil, nor does he tempt anyone; but each one is tempted when, by his own evil desire, he is dragged away and enticed. Then, after desire has conceived, it gives birth to sin; and sin, when it is full-grown, **gives birth to death**. James 1:13-15(NIV)

We live as a society of individuals. When any one of us selfishly take from or harm someone else for our own selfish benefit, we all suffer. If our society of mankind does not have life, then every individual loses out. And when an individual sins, he affects all of society, because we were created by God; as social creatures, to need one another and to live together in harmony. Sin destroys that harmony. Sexual sin is not different. God gave us sex as a very beautiful and important part of his creation. But when we use it in a perverted manner, we bring about death to us all in the long-run. *This lesson is not meant to lay down the law about how guilty we are of sexual sins. The purpose is to see that sexual sin is damaging to us individually, to others, to society as a whole, and to our Creator who created male and female and sex as a beautiful thing and who is the source of all life, and desires for us to have his life through his design for the sexual union and marriage.*

What is a sexual sin? Why is sex outside of marriage so bad? Why isn't all sex good if there is pleasure and satisfaction? Why should it matter what happens in my own personal privacy? Who does it hurt? Why should there be age limits on who has sex?

I grew up with an older brother who introduced me to pornography and masturbation before I was ten years old. From this early age one of my main drives in life was sexual pleasure. All of these questions—those were mine at the time. I wasn't asking questions, looking for answers; I was promoting freedom for sexual activity. Pornography, daily masturbation, sex with countless women, filthy talk and continual lust for every attractive woman I saw—that was me. And I saw absolutely nothing wrong with it.

I married at twenty five, and within weeks of marriage I told my wife that I could not see myself remaining sexually faithful to her, but not to worry, I would still love her. I did not equate my faithless lusts with my lack of love for her. And the pornography, the masturbation and lust continued.

I had a beautiful wife, and I was an ignorant fool who was a slave to my sexual flesh. I had no idea that I was planting the seeds of destruction for myself, my marriage, my children, my wife and society. My sexual prowess and promiscuity did not make me a "man"; it made me a perverted sinner.

You see, God has designed the sexual union to be pure between a man and a woman in marriage.

Marriage should be honored by all, and the marriage bed kept pure, for God will judge the adulterer and all the sexually immoral. Hebrews 13:4(NIV)

Like all of God's laws and commands, they are given for our good. We were created to live in a certain manner. When we violate that living design, we reap death. In essence, sin is a killer; it is spiritual poison.

For the **wages of sin is death**, but the gift of God is eternal life in Christ Jesus our Lord. Romans 6:23(NIV)

The sexual union is meant to be very beautiful—physically and spiritually. The devil wants to destroy this beauty and us. He uses lies, our sinful desires, our wounded hearts, our ignorance and the depravity of others to pervert and destroy this wonderful beauty of sex between a husband and wife.

I acted in ignorance in my younger years. God saved me from this ignorance just in time. I have been faithful to my wife of 44 years, and my marriage is happy and satisfying. If I had continued in the way that I was headed, I would have been divorced long ago. I would have children living without their father. My drive for sexual fulfillment would still not be satisfied. *Free sex never fully satisfies*. I probably would have become a sexually active, disturbed and unhappy man with lots of people casualties along my wayward paths.

I was not the only one who lived like this. Many men have sown the seeds of destruction, and we have created divorced mothers, children of divorce, children out-of-wedlock, many broken family relationships, financial tragedy and more—all this due to ignorance and ignorant behavior.

So I tell you this, and insist on it in the Lord, that you must no longer live as the Gentiles do, in the futility of their thinking. They are darkened in their understanding and separated from the life of God because of the ignorance that is in them due to the hardening of their hearts. Ephesians 4:17-18(NIV)

It doesn't take much reasoning to understand why God set boundaries around sex, but I didn't want to hear any of it. I was enjoying my sexual freedom, and I didn't want to hear the simple truths.

We will talk in more detail about some of these perversions in future lessons, but let's quickly go through some of these perversions to identify the destructive behavior.

- Fornication: Practicing the sexual union outside of the marriage union. This is a perverted violation of God's intensions for this union. It has the likelihood of producing children outside of a family. It produces a cultural temptation for others to practice sex outside of marriage. And once practiced, it tempts the married husband or wife to lust after others and to become unfaithful in their marriage.
- Adultery: The theft of what belongs to another man. She is his wife, and I am having sex with her.
- Prostitution: The sale of a woman's body for financial gain. It makes the woman undesirable for marriage. Children are born without a family to raise them. The prostitute is drained of any self-worth and typically goes through life completely damaged on the inside. The man loses self-respect and cripples his ability to have a prosperous relationship with a wife. Sexually transmitted diseases rapidly spread, and he likely will plague his life with a disease that may kill him and others. (Similar consequences are also true for male prostitutes.)
- Abortion: The willful murder of an unwanted child. 83% of abortions are by unwed mothers. Abortion does not make the woman unpregnant; it makes her the mother of a dead baby. Instead of giving life, she took it. The men who get them pregnant many times push for the abortion.

- Rape: Where adultery is consensual, rape is stealing directly from a woman without her consent. She may be physically harmed, but the greater wound is to her inner being. The scars last a lifetime and can forever damage her future relationship with men.

- Incest: Sex with close relatives, such as our sister or daughter. There are laws against even marrying these close relatives due to the potential of having genetic defects. But the reasoning goes beyond genetics. Sexual relationships go far beyond the physical uniting of two bodies. Sex is the final outcome of a spiritual unity between a man and a woman in marriage. In this life that God has created, there are many types of relationships. We are to honor each one accordingly. For example, brothers and sisters have a special family relationship, and are not to have sex with each other. Nor are we to sleep with our mother or mother-in-law.

"Cursed is the man who sleeps with his father's wife, for he dishonors his father's bed." Then all the people shall say, "Amen!" Deuteronomy 27:20(NIV)

"Cursed is the man who sleeps with his mother-in-law." Then all the people shall say, "Amen!" Deuteronomy 27:23

"Cursed is the man who sleeps with his sister, the daughter of his father or the daughter of his mother." Then all the people shall say, "Amen!" Deuteronomy 27:22(NIV)

- Pedophilia: Sex with young children is a form of rape. It is not consensual, although consent may be given out of fear, confusion, the demands of one in authority, a false identity of love and care, forced sexual pleasure or innocence. These acts are most commonly performed by an adult that is in a position of love, trust and authority, such as a parent, uncle, pastor or close family friend. These acts, which are typically repetitive, destroy the child's healthy sexual identity and destroy his or her understanding of true love and trust, since they were performed by someone who should have loved him or her.

- Bestiality: Sex was created to be experienced between a married man and woman. Any other type of sex is a perversion of God's creation. Sex with animals is a sexual experience with no possibility for a spiritual union and degrades marriage, the only place created for such a union.

"Cursed is the man who has sexual relations with any animal." Then all the people shall say, "Amen!" Deuteronomy 27:21(NIV)

Do not have sexual relations with an animal and defile yourself with it. A woman must not present herself to an animal to have sexual relations with it; **that is a perversion**. Leviticus 18:23(NIV)

- Homosexuality: Sex with the same sex is also a perversion of God's original creation of man, woman and marriage. However, it is no more of a perversion than the many other sexual perversions mentioned.

Do not lie with a man as one lies with a woman; that is detestable. Leviticus 18:22(NIV)

The temptations to homosexuality for those with this identity are <u>not</u> sin. Acting out our temptations is sin. Heterosexuals have temptations too. For example, a man may be sexually tempted by looking at a beautiful woman. If he lusts for her, he has sinned. If he flees from his lust, he has not sinned. (Matthew 5:27-30) Similarly, the temptations of someone with homosexual tendencies are not sin, but allowing one's self to ponder in lust is sin. And clearly, the pursuit and acting out of homosexual behavior is sin. But the mere fact that someone may have sexual attractions for the same sex is not sin as long as he refrains from lust and homosexual acts. The outward promotion of homosexuality is an attack on God's order for man

40

and woman. God will give those over to their sin who promote a lie about what God created.

Therefore God gave them over in the sinful desires of their hearts to sexual impurity for the degrading of their bodies with one another. They exchanged the truth of God for a lie, and worshiped and served created things rather than the Creator—who is forever praised. Amen.

Because of this, God gave them over to shameful lusts. Even their women exchanged natural relations for unnatural ones. In the same way the men also abandoned natural relations with women and were inflamed with lust for one another. Men committed indecent acts with other men, and received in themselves the due penalty for their perversion.

Furthermore, since they did not think it worthwhile to retain the knowledge of God, he gave them over to a depraved mind, to do what ought not to be done. Romans 1:24-28(NIV)

The homosexual identity will be discussed in more depth in a later lesson.

The sexual union between a husband and wife is a beautiful creation of God. Within this union come enormous blessings, not just during the sexual act, but the entire relationship. And from this relationship the family is derived. And from this family godly children are raised. And from these godly children come godly adults that rule the earth as God commanded man from the beginning. The destruction of the godly sexual union between husband and wife is the destruction of all society by striking at the roots. This is why there has been such a fierce attack upon this union by the devil and the world culture which he controls. We have to be very wise and careful not to raise up deviant sexual behavior as good. This has been done with most all of the sins listed above. But look at what the Scriptures say.

Woe to those who call evil good and good evil, who put darkness for light and light for darkness, who put bitter for sweet and sweet for bitter. Isaiah 5:20(NIV)

Is this not what has happened with the sexual union today?

Reflection questions

How do sexual sins destroy us individually?

How do they wound others?

How do they infect our society as a whole?

What has been your experience in these areas?

Chapter Seven

Our Identity

There is a psychology term called imprinting. Imprinting has to do with the identity of animals with human beings. For example, when a baby duck is taken from his mother and raised by human beings as a pet, without the presence of other ducks, the duck follows the owner around just as it would have done with its own mother. The duck was born a duck and looks like a duck. In all practical terms, it is a duck. However, the duck has identified with its new mother, and the duck sees itself as a human being. That is called imprinting, a common psychology term for the misplaced identity of animals with their owners.

If a baby animal is taken out of the wild, say a young fawn. The fawn cannot be raised to maturity as a domestic animal and then put it back out into the wild. It may have all the biological character and instincts of a wild animal, but the deer has not been exposed to the wild habitat. It does not identify itself with the wild. It identifies itself with a domestic existence. If it does reenter the wild environment, it has to be very slow with a gradual introduction of the wild and a gradual removal of the domestic provisions and protection. The deer is very vulnerable during this transition.

What does this have to do with us? We, too, have identities based upon the circumstances of our upbringing. We have all sorts of identities. We even identify with sports teams. When "our" team wins, we feel like a winner. When "our" team loses, we may even become angry or depressed over the loss. We may identify with a team that is hundreds of miles away. We may not know one player personally. But when they are winners, we feel like winners.

Identity is a mysterious and complex spiritual component of every living person. We were created with a need to have identities. However, like all other aspects of our created being, our identities can become distorted, unhealthy and perverted. Instead of bringing us prosperity and blessings, the distortions can bring us down. They can disappoint us and lead us down a path of destruction. It is critically important to know our identities. Jesus came so that we could see, repent, change and seek his life, which is the only true life.

Sexual Identity

We take on all sorts of identities. For example, when men gather together, they may naturally tend to talk about their job or career because their perceived worth is found in their work. Woman will typically begin talking about their children and grandchildren because they identify themselves as mothers. We may identify with our possessions, so we want others to see our car or our house or our clothing. We may identify with our bodies, so a man may show off his muscular build, or a woman may show off her beauty or figure. Men tend to see themselves as macho, so they talk about sports and their masculine hobbies. Women, on the other hand, generally see their femininity, and they identify with nurturing, cooking and making their home warm and beautiful. There are all sorts of identities. Not every male or every female fits the same mold, but we all have identities that define who we are inside.

How we perceive ourselves sexually is a major area of identity. We all have our sexual identities. However, the roles of men and women in our society have been perverted and distorted such that we have to rediscover the true identity that God has established for his creation. Who are we as

44

men? What distinguishes men from women? Let's go back to the beginning, before sin and corruption (Read Genesis 2:15-22).

The man was created to rule over, to work, to take care of God's marvelous, beautiful creation. The woman was not created to do his work, but to be a helper in his work. Notice also that the man was commanded not to eat of the tree of the knowledge of good and evil, not the woman. She was not even created at this point. It is the man's responsibility to get the work done. It was man's responsibility to stay clear of the forbidden fruit. After sin, God put a curse on the man and the woman, and they were different curses. However, their disobedience was related. Eve took Adam's place of rule and Adam did not take his place of leading and protection.

Then he said to the woman, "I will sharpen the pain of your pregnancy, and in pain you will give birth. And **you will desire to control your husband, but he will rule over you.**"

And to the man he said, "**Since you listened to your wife and ate from the tree whose fruit I commanded you not to eat, the ground is cursed because of you.** All your life you will struggle to scratch a living from it.

It will grow thorns and thistles for you, though you will eat of its grains. By the sweat of your brow will you have food to eat until you return to the ground from which you were made. For you were made from dust, and to dust you will return." Genesis 3:16-19 (NLT)

The woman was cursed because she did not allow her husband to lead, and her curse was that her husband would rule over her. The man was cursed because he listened to his wife. He was supposed to be in charge, to be obedient to God's commands, to protect his wife in all things. But he didn't. He laid back; let his wife go ahead and lead, and he followed her right into sin.

Sexual identity goes far beyond what we look like in the nude. It encompasses our understanding of our God-given responsibilities and character. A sign of a degraded society is one where these roles become turned around; where a woman identifies with the man's role and the man identifies with the woman's role. Isaiah wrote about such a disgraceful time as this.

Youths oppress my people, women rule over them. O my people, your guides lead you astray; they turn you from the path. Isaiah 3:12(NIV)

Isaiah then prophesied that God would humble the women with shame. Then they would seek out a man to submit to in order to remove the disgrace that they brought upon themselves by the haughty behavior of raising themselves above men.

In that day seven women will take hold of one man and say, "We will eat our own food and provide our own clothes; only let us be called by your name. Take away our disgrace!" Isaiah 4:1

This is not just a problem regarding the women of today. It starts with men. Remember, Adam could have stopped Eve's foolish behavior at any time, but he willfully chose to eat of the forbidden fruit at Eve's command. Our attitude and behavior has not changed much. Far too many men today treat their wives as their mothers, expecting them to care for their every physical need as well as the children. Men act like little boys in men's bodies and with men's play.

On the flip side, women go off to work and become the main breadwinner. Women even go to war today, wearing a man's uniform and carrying a man's artillery. Men have to compete with women in all of the places that were once regarded as men's roles.

The roles of men and women are not clear any more. They have become clouded with our cultural norms, expectations and even laws. Men and women have lost their God-given identities. We have lost the recipe

46

for God' original creation, which was designed to prosper in beauty. It is no longer prosperous, and it is no longer beautiful.

Born Male, but the Identity Is Developed

We are born male and female. Each one of us men can look at our sexual parts and our sex becomes quite obvious. There are many aspects of our character that come at birth that can drive us to behave in a masculine or feminine behavior. Boys tend to be more rambunctious and physical. Boys tend to be less relational than girls. These differences may be seen right from birth, but not always. The naturally born character of boys or girls may drive us toward a male or female identity, but they should not be confused with identity. We were not born with a sexual identity. That was developed after we were born. For most of us, that identity was established in the first few years of our life and was reinforced into our adolescent years.

For boys, we began our life in our mother's womb. We heard her voice and felt her protection and warmth before we were even born. From birth, most of us were nurtured by our mother. She is the one who spent the most time holding us and feeding us. Many of us were nursed and fell asleep in her arms.

But this time does not last long. In less than a year we began to pull away from all this time with mom. There was a world outside of her arms to explore. In a good home, dad was present during those times, and his strong arms were also holding and caressing us. Just the size of dad and the tone of his voice made him so much different than mom. From about one year of age to about three we move away from the constant care of mom and begin to explore the world around us for ourselves. We begin forming other relationships with our brothers and sisters, but most importantly with dad.

This time is most critical for forming our sexual identity. It is complex. Are we surrounded by older sisters or older brothers, or are we an only child? How much time is spent with Dad, or is he absent. Who is Dad? Is Mom the one who is strong and runs the household, while Dad is weak and passive? As a boy, does he want to identify with his passive, weak father or his dominant strong mother?

What if Dad wasn't passive? What if he was very masculine and you also had older brothers who were very rough and tumble—obviously Dad's favorites. What if you were smaller, weaker, less coordinated and not prone to sports or heavy physical activity? How would this affect your sexual identity? Who would you favor, Mom or Dad?

What if Dad was angry and mean, and he abused you and your siblings and Mom, and during these times Mom was your protector? Would you be drawn to identify with Dad or Mom?

We live in a sinful world. Every parent that has ever lived—from Adam and Eve until now—has been a sinner. All of us were born into sinful families and were raised by sinful parents. We, too, are sinners. Our identity with Mom and Dad has affected our entire character—how we see others, how we see the world, how we see our heavenly Father and how we see ourselves. This identity influences every one of our relationships. It affects our sexual identity. As already discussed, sex goes far beyond our sexual organs and having an organism. It goes far beyond male and female. It cannot be separated from the loving relationships we had with our parents. And it cannot be separated from every relationship we have had with people in general—male or female.

What if we experienced regular sexually abuse by our father, or by our mother? How does that distort our view of the sexual union? How does it distort the view of marriage? How does it distort the view of a father or the view of a mother? How does it distort the view of our own identity? How does it make us angry? How does it affect our view of life and our behavior?

If Dad was strong and loving, we will identify with him for his love and strength. If he was angry and abusive, we, too, may become angry and abusive, but we may not identify with him because of our fear of him. We may identify more with Mom, and when we are older we may seek out a wife to become a substitute mom. We may even seek out a man to be a substitute dad, since we never had a loving dad for identity, and we all long for a loving dad. This is so important to recognize; we all have a God-given need to have a strong loving dad. All of our dads have fallen short of this role because of sin, and so have we. But that does not change our inner, heartfelt need for a right relationship with Dad. We may spend the rest of our lives trying to find such a substitute.

This can be true for girls or boys. A young girl longs for her dad's love and protection. She is blessed by his strength and his love for her mom. But what if her dad is abusive to her mom? What if her mom is seen as a trapped, weak victim? This little girl may grow up never wanting to be like her mom. She may not want to be like her dad either, but at least her dad was not the abused victim. Now her sexual identity may become perverted.

These many scenarios can become very complex and difficult to discern. We cannot just look into our heart and soul and see all that has gone on in our past and to see all of the wounds, the fears and the misinterpretations and perceptions. We may not be able to see deep inside ourselves, but that is the place that drives our identities, feelings and outward behaviors.

Identity with Christ and our Heavenly Father

My dad was harsh and mostly disinterested in us kids. When I came to the Lord at about 30 years of age, I longed to see my dad come to him also so that we could share a close relationship together that we never had. I was a very physical kid with an older brother, so my male identity was well established, but my missing relationship with my father was still deep within my heart. Our reunion never happened; he died. God showed me that he was a saved man just as I. He also showed me that my father was a man just like I, with all the physical and emotional struggles of life. I never saw that in him until after his death. I have also come to realize that every father is imperfect. Our hope is not in the pursuit of our earthly father's love. Certainly, any reconciliation between a son and his dad is a good thing. But that is not where security is found. Ultimately, our security rests in the protection and care of our loving heavenly Father. He is perfect in all ways. He is the source of all wisdom and knowledge. God is love. He understands what goes on in our hearts better than we do. God is the answer to all of our emotional struggles. And he sent his Holy Spirit to live within us, to experience everything that we think and feel, all of our pain and all of our sin and all of our anger and all of our frustrations. He lives within us to restore us and to set our feet upon a solid foundation—Jesus Christ.

How many of us see ourselves as worthless, dirty and rejected? How many of us see ourselves as unrighteous? It is fully possible to rid ourselves of our old decrepit identity and put on a new wholesome identity. If our lives have been on a destructive road, we may identify ourselves as lost, worthless, dirty, sinful, rejected and generally less than others. However, when we come to Christ, our past is wiped clean and we take on a new identity, that of Christ. He gives us his very own Spirit to live within us, and we are now like Jesus. We have become sons of God with a new father, our heavenly Father.

For you died, and your life is now hidden with Christ in God. Colossians 3:3(NIV)

I have been crucified with Christ and I no longer live, but Christ lives in me. The life I live in the body, I live by faith in the Son of God, who loved me and gave himself for me. Galatians 2:20(NIV)

Therefore, if anyone is in Christ, he is a new creation; the old has gone, the new has come! 2 Corinthians 5:17(NIV)

Our true and lasting identity should be with the one and only complete man, Jesus Christ. When we know him, we know our heavenly Father.

Jesus answered, "I am the way and the truth and the life. No one comes to the Father except through me. If you really knew me, you would know my Father as well. From now on, you do know him and have seen him." John 14:6-7(NIV)

Reflection questions

Was your father the provider and protector of his wife and children? How are you like your father?

Describe Jesus as a man.

How do you look to your wife as a mother to you?

Besides your physical being, what identifies you as being a man? (If you are a woman, what identifies you as a woman?)

What are your identities? (Think about sports, education/intellectual, cool, job/career, house, cars, dress, friends/family/group/gang, organization, behavior style, deviant behavior.)

Are you a child of God by receiving the Spirit of God? Describe your new identity in Christ? How has your new identity changed your perception of yourself?

Chapter Eight

Adultery

Adultery is the act of having intercourse with a married man or woman who is not your spouse. In every adulterous affair there is an adulterer and an adulteress. Both commit adultery. It could be that both the man and the woman are married to someone else. It could be that one or the other is married to someone else. Sexual intercourse is reserved by God to be between a man and woman who are married to each other. Anyone who violates this principle commits adultery.

Who Owns Who? Adultery Is Theft.

Marriage is the unity of a man and a woman performed by God. In this unity the man's body belongs to himself and to his wife. The wife's body belongs to herself and to her husband.

> The wife's body does not belong to her alone but also to her husband. In the same way, the husband's body does not belong to him alone but also to his wife. 1 Corinthians 7:4(NIV)

Adultery is the act of giving away what belongs to our spouse. It is also the act of the other party of taking something that does not belong to him/her. In other words, adultery is theft on the part of both parties. It is the act of taking something that is not yours for your own selfish pleasure.

When you see a **thief**, you join with him; you throw in your lot with **adulterers**. Psalm 50:18(NIV)

For the commandments are like a lamp, instruction is like a light, and rebukes of discipline are like the road leading to life, by keeping you from the evil woman, from the smooth tongue of the loose woman. **Do not lust in your heart for her beauty, and do not let her captivate you with her alluring eyes**; for on account of a prostitute one is brought down to a loaf of bread, but **the wife of another man preys on your precious life**. Can a man hold fire against his chest without burning his clothes? Can a man walk on hot coals without scorching his feet? **So it is with the one who has sex with his neighbor's wife; no one who touches her will escape punishment**. People do not despise a thief when he steals to fulfill his need when he is hungry. Yet if he is caught he must repay seven times over, he might even have to give all the wealth of his house. **A man who commits adultery with a woman lacks wisdom, whoever does it destroys his own life. He will be beaten and despised, and his reproach will not be wiped away; for jealousy kindles a husband's rage, and he will not show mercy when he takes revenge. He will not consider any compensation; he will not be willing, even if you multiply the compensation.** Proverbs 6:23-35(NET)

It is not our right to sleep with another man or woman's spouse. And it is not our right to give our body to another, since our body belongs to our spouse. God clearly commands us not to commit adultery and not to steal.

You shall not commit adultery. You shall not steal. Exodus 20:14-15(NIV)

When single men commit adultery, they are stealing the wife of another man. When married men commit adultery, they may be stealing from another man if the woman is married. But even if she is not, they have committed adultery because what he has given to another woman belonged exclusively to his wife. To put it bluntly, nakedness belongs to a married husband and wife with no exceptions. In the case of an adulterous husband, when he gives his naked body to another woman, he has stolen from his own wife what belongs to her and her alone. The pleasure the strange woman received from him was the pleasure reserved for his wife. The pleasure received is a pleasure that blesses the woman. This blessing should only be experienced by our wives. A man's sexual pleasure belongs to his wife, and her sexual pleasure belongs to her husband. That is God's design for the sexual union. Any other practice is adultery, which is selfish theft.

Adultery Is a Grievous Sin

All sin is grievous. All sin leads to death and needs the atonement by the blood of Christ Jesus. But if we continue to walk in wickedness—and adultery is wickedness—we are in danger of the fire of hell. Jesus was very clear on this matter.

> You have heard that it was said, 'Do not commit adultery.' But I tell you that anyone who looks at a woman lustfully has already committed adultery with her in her heart. If your right eye causes you to sin, gouge it out and throw it away. It is better for you to lose one part of your body than for **your whole body to be thrown into hell**. Matthew 5:27-29(NIV)

If we confess that Jesus is Lord, we must turn from wickedness so that our actions bear truth to our confession of the Lord.

Nevertheless, God's solid foundation stands firm, sealed with this inscription: "The Lord knows those who are his," and, "**Everyone who confesses the name of the Lord must turn away from wickedness.**" 2 Timothy 2:19(NIV)

Adultery is clearly wickedness, and those who do not repent of their adultery will not inherit eternal life in the kingdom of God.

Do you not know that **the wicked will not inherit the kingdom of God**? Do not be deceived: **Neither the sexually immoral** nor idolaters nor **adulterers** nor **male prostitutes** nor **homosexual offenders** nor **thieves** nor the greedy nor drunkards nor slanderers nor swindlers **will inherit the kingdom of G**od. 1 Corinthians 6:9-10(NIV)
(Also read Galatians 5:19-21, Ephesians 5:3-5, Revelation 21:8, 22:15, Matthew 5:27-29, Hebrews 11:24-25, 4:15)

Adultery Is a Trap

Sexual temptations are very strong—maybe as strong as any drug addiction. Once tempted—once turned on—it is very difficult to turn away. The Scriptures strongly warn us to flee the temptation of the adulteress woman.

For the lips of an adulteress drip honey, and her speech is smoother than oil; but in the end she is bitter as gall, sharp as a double-edged sword. Her feet go down to death; her steps lead straight to the grave. She gives no thought to the way of life; her paths are crooked, but she knows it not. Proverbs 5:3-6(NIV)

Why be captivated, my son, by an adulteress? Why embrace the bosom of another man's wife? Proverbs 5:20(NIV)

Do not lust in your heart after her beauty or let her captivate you with her eyes, for **the prostitute reduces you to a loaf of bread, and the adulteress preys upon your very life.** Can a man scoop fire into his lap without his clothes being burned? Can a man walk on hot coals without his feet being scorched? So is he who sleeps with another man's wife; no one who touches her will go unpunished. Proverbs 6:25-29(NIV)

We seek out a woman who desires to sleep with us because we think we will derive enormous sexual pleasure. It is the anticipation of this fleshly delight that sucks us in to the trap. We all must be convicted of the enormity of this sin and make a decision long before we are tempted that we will not play with this temptation. Play begins long before the act. Adultery begins in the heart. That is the place of battle.

For out of the heart come evil thoughts, murder, **adultery, sexual immorality**, theft, false testimony, slander. Matthew 15:19(NIV)

We have to make a decision to flee any temptation before we are tempted. If not, we may get taken in and taken down. It is much better to judge our own hearts for lust and flirtations before God judges our hearts and our actions.

Marriage should be honored by all, and **the marriage bed kept pure**, for **God will judge the adulterer and all the sexually immoral**. Hebrews 13:4(NIV)

Reflection questions

Have you confessed and repented of your lust for another woman?

How do you flee the temptations?

Are you accountable and honest with anyone about your sexual behavior and fantasies?

Chapter Nine

Pornography

Pornography has become a ten to fourteen billion dollar industry. It is an industry that preys upon men and women. It has taken a beautiful creation of God and exploits her nakedness for profit. Women submit to having their naked bodies and open sexual acts photographed and video recorded so that the pictures and movies can be sold to strange men who will use the naked exposure to fanaticize about having a private sexual experience. Women submit to this exposure for the money they receive. Men give their money for the pleasure of getting a sexual arousal and climax. For men and women, it is all about money and the sinful fleshly pleasure. For the devil, it is all about degrading, perverting and corrupting one of God's most beautiful creations and for the destruction of marriage and the family. Like drugs, pornography leads to addiction and control of its victim.

Although pornography is primarily for men, women pursue it for similar reasons. Pornography is a substitute for a physical sexual relationship, but it is not innocent just because there is no actual physical contact. The destructive effects can be just as severe as an adulterous affair.

Pornography is not just for the single man. The single man may justify his behavior because he is not married and he thinks he needs an outlet for his sexual drives. Married men are just as likely to pursue pornography, with devastating effects to himself, his marriage and family.

Researcher Patrick Fagan, PhD, a psychologist and former Deputy Assistant Health and Human Services Secretary, calls pornography a "quiet family killer" and says it is time for citizens to buck the laissez-faire approach to porn. His key findings:

- Pornography use was correlated with an increase in infidelity of more than 300%. (Other factors may have also contributed to the infidelity, but it was a factor.)
- 56% of divorces involved one party having an obsessive interest in porn.
- Married men who are involved in pornography feel less sexually satisfied with their spouse and less attached to her. Wives notice and are upset by the difference. Many wives begin to feel unattractive or sexually inadequate.
- More than half of those engaged in cybersex lost interest in sexual intercourse; one-third of their partners also lost interest.
- Pornography is addictive, and neuroscientists are beginning to map the biological substrate.
- Users become desensitized and tend to seek more extreme types of pornography (including viewing aggressive behaviors and rape).
- Child-sex offenders are more likely to distribute or regularly view pornography.
- Pornography use alters sexual attitudes and behavior.
- Adolescents exposed to high levels of pornography use had lower levels of sexual self-esteem. Porn use was highly correlated with increased sex with non-romantic friends.
- Men are six times more likely to view pornography as females, and spend more time viewing it. However, among women who engaged in cybersex, 80% went on to have real-life sexual affairs, compared to 33% of men.

- When brains are scanned using a PET scanner while viewing pornography, the brain reactions are similar to a cocaine addict's brain while viewing images of others using cocaine.
- The presence of sexually oriented businesses in communities leads to increases in crime and decreases in property rates.
- Dr. Fagan concludes, "Pornography corrodes the conscience, promotes distrust between husbands and wives and debases untold thousands of young women. It is not harmless escapism but relational and emotional poison."[1]

Pornography is the modern day ability to have multiple sex partners—hundreds, even thousands. God warned Solomon not to pursue wives from foreign nations, but Solomon ignored God's warning, and it became his downfall.

King Solomon, however, loved many foreign women besides Pharaoh's daughter—Moabites, Ammonites, Edomites, Sidonians and Hittites. They were from nations about which the LORD had told the Israelites, "You must not intermarry with them, because they will surely turn your hearts after their gods." Nevertheless, Solomon held fast to them in love. **He had seven hundred wives of royal birth and three hundred concubines, and his wives led him astray.** As Solomon grew old, his wives turned his heart after other gods, and his heart was not fully devoted to the LORD his God, as the heart of David his father had been. He followed Ashtoreth the goddess of the Sidonians, and Molech the detestable god of the Ammonites. So Solomon did evil in the eyes of the LORD; he did not follow the LORD completely, as David his father had done. 1 Kings 11:1-6(NIV)

---

[1] Patrick F. Fagan, PhD, *The Effects of Pornography on Individuals, Marriage, Family and Community*, co-published by the Family Research Council in Washington D.C. and the Marriage and Religion Institute (MARRI), December, 2009.

Solomon was a rich and powerful king. He did not need multiple wives, but his flesh craved to be satisfied, and he gave into its demands. The draw to pornography is a similar temptation with a similar warning and downfall for us.

No man needs a thousand wives and lovers. So how many does he need? Two? Five? Ten? Surely ten would be enough. But if we consider pornography, there are never enough women to satisfy. Possessing multiple women is a fantasy that we chase. It is the carrot on the end of a stick that is always just ahead of us, so we keep running farther and farther, faster and faster. But the final pleasure is never quite satisfied like we thought. There always has to be more. *The fantasy controls us; we do not control the fantasy.* Eventually it takes us down. It destroys us and our marriage. Instead of being more satisfied, we develop an appetite that is impossible to fill. In the end we look for more and more, but more is not there.

Pornography Is a Trap

The Bible talks about being a slave to our flesh. No one wants to be a slave. Who wants to have someone or something control our behavior? But look at the Scriptures.

> Don't you know that when you offer yourselves to someone to obey him as slaves, you are slaves to the one whom you obey—whether you are **slaves to sin**, which **leads to death**, or to **obedience**, which **leads to righteousness**? Romans 6:16(NIV)

> I put this in human terms because you are weak in your natural selves. **Just as you used to offer the parts of your body in slavery to impurity and to ever-increasing wickedness, so now offer them in slavery to righteousness leading to holiness.** When you were slaves to sin, you were free from the control of righteousness. What benefit did you reap

at that time from the things you are now ashamed of? Those things result in death! But now that you have been set free from sin and have become slaves to God, the benefit you reap leads to holiness, and the result is eternal life. For the wages of sin is death, but the gift of God is eternal life in Christ Jesus our Lord. Romans 6:19-23(NIV)

The drive to seek out the sexual stimulation of pornography comes from the sinful nature within us. Like most drives of the flesh, there is pleasure in it. This pleasure is very deceiving. It promises life. It lies to us and tells us that this momentary pleasure is good and that we will find fulfillment in it. The fulfillment is short-lived, but that does not clue us to the deception. We believe that we can just keep seeking more and more, and it will get better and better. It is much like the temptation to take drugs. It gives a great satisfaction that does not last, and it is always back at our door, demanding another taste, but this time a little more.

We are deceived into thinking we are getting what we want, so we are in control. But the truth is that it controls us. We are not free. We find that the more we engage, the more we have to seek the temptation. We actually enjoy the temptation, and we enjoy being possessed by it.

We are fooled into thinking, "Who does it harm?" What we do not see is that it has taken us captive. We do not see that it is dragging us down a private road. Married men do not engage in this lustful activity in the full knowledge of their wives. They secretly get on the internet when their wife is in bed or away from home. They get themselves all turned on so they can go off by themselves and masturbate over their lustful fantasies. They commit adultery in their hearts on a daily basis, thinking their spouse doesn't know, so how can it hurt her.

"You have heard that it was said, 'Do not commit adultery.' But I tell you that anyone who looks at a woman lustfully has already committed adultery with her in his heart. If your right eye causes you to sin, gouge it out and throw it away. It is better for you to lose one

part of your body than for your whole body to be thrown into hell. And if your right hand causes you to sin, cut it off and throw it away. It is better for you to lose one part of your body than for your whole body to go into hell. Matthew 5:27-30(NIV)

Every Man's Battle, Arterburn & Stoeker, is an excellent study for overcoming our sexual temptations to sin. The title hits the nail on the head; this is every man's battle. We are all turned on by the looks and the thoughts of a beautiful woman's body. But just because we are all tempted—normal—doesn't mean that it must be right. We all have a sinful nature. Sin is normal among men, but sin is also a killer among men, with no exceptions. It is a sin common enough and important enough to God that it is listed as one of the Ten Commandments.

You shall not covet your neighbor's house. **You shall not covet your neighbor's wife, or his manservant or maidservant**, his ox or donkey, or anything that belongs to your neighbor." Exodus 20:17(NIV)

Coveting is something that we do in our mind and heart. There may not be any physical action; it is all internal. This leads us to believe that there is no sin. We tend to believe that what goes on inside of us is private and harms no one. Our thoughts belong to us, so they should not come under judgment. I can do what I want with myself. Even masturbation is private. It's my body, so I should be able to do what I want with it. Who does it harm? But that is not how Jesus sees our lustful thoughts (see Matthew 5:27-30 above).

Sin begins in the heart. It starts at the inner core of our being. Then it works its way to the outside. Just because it is still on the inside does not make it innocent.

When tempted, no one should say, "God is tempting me." For God cannot be tempted by evil, nor does he tempt anyone; but each one is tempted when, by **his own evil desire, he is dragged away and enticed. Then, after desire has conceived, it gives birth to sin; and sin, when it is full-grown, gives birth to death.** James 1:13-15(NIV)

Temptation begins in the heart and mind. Satisfying our sexual drives with pornography and masturbation is a practice that we hide from others. We seek it out in darkness, hiding it from others. The married man pursues it without his wife's knowledge because he knows that he is sinning against her. He goes off and masturbates over his fantasies of other women, cheating his wife of his desire for just her. Men who continue down this lustful road usually end up divorced. His private lust costs him his marriage. And it cost his wife and children much more. He is a cheat and a thief. His damage to his wife, children and society goes far beyond his imagination. Sexual purity is a requirement for strong healthy families. Strong healthy families are a requirement for a stable, strong and prosperous society and nation. *Satan can destroy a nation through the lust of men!*

Just think of how degrading pornography is to the women who pose naked before men around the world; men who fulfill their sexual pleasures as they stare at women's private sexual parts. This fulfillment usually is not confined to just the view. Men stare at these naked figures as they fanaticize and masturbate. This is what women subject their naked bodies to when they pose for pornography. God created the nakedness of a woman for the pleasure of her husband. Participating in the sins of pornography is a direct insult to and offense against God.

Job knew of his own temptations, and he knew of the offense to God. He made a choice; a choice to deny his eyes the pleasure of a lustful look at another woman.

I made a covenant with my eyes not to look lustfully at a girl. For what is man's lot from God above, his heritage from the Almighty on high? Is it not ruin for the wicked, disaster for those who do wrong? **Does he not see my ways and count my every step?** Job 31:1-4(NIV)

Job knew that his thoughts were not truly private. God can see every one of them. When we go off alone and get ourselves all turned on over the naked pictures of women. When we fulfill our hormonal drives and pleasures—God sees our every thought, feelings and actions. Nothing is hidden from him.

Sexual temptations are a trap. Like any good trap, there is a progressive lure. As James described (above)

1. By our own evil desire, we are dragged away and enticed.
2. Then, after desire has conceived, it gives birth to sin
3. sin, when it is full-grown, gives birth to death

In the case of sexual temptation it might go like this:

1. First, an unintentional or intentional look, and we are aroused.
2. Intentionally look again and allow it to turn us on through a fantasy.
3. Pursuit of ownership for a longer engaged look.
4. Fantasy with masturbation.
5. Go back for a deeper, more involved view with a deeper more involved fantasy.
6. Adultery of the heart pursues the real thing.
7. Unfaithfulness has already brought damage to the marriage, now divorce sets in.

The first look may be a magazine, a movie, the internet, etc. It may be a look at a woman in public, friend or stranger. It may progress to an intentional next step—a conversation, an intimate complement. Then it may go further with a personal conversation, followed by scheduled time together, such as lunch. Then more communication and longer more private time together. Then touch. Then intimate touch. Then sex.

Pornography is a trap that will take us captive to sexual sin. Victory comes by denying the smallest temptation. Otherwise, it will progress to a point where the temptation is more than we can handle.

Reflection questions

Do you consistently bounce your eyes away from a tempting look?

Do you regularly turn yourself on with intentional fantasies?

Have you maintained your media standards (no porn pictures, TV, etc.)?

Do you routinely masturbate?

Chapter Ten

Filthy Language, Dress and Habits

Our culture is designed to degrade the beauty of the sexual union. It cheapens this union and presents it as a commodity, something to be marketed, used for marketing and the means of drawing attention. The possibilities are endless, and the degrading exposure seems to be endless.

Foul Mouths

Our words are very weighty, even the words that we use that have no apparent intent or purpose, such as swearing. All sorts of profanity are spoken where the words are just extra expressions added to our sentences. For the most part, they have nothing to do with the main thought. Most of these words can be divided into two categories: One, taking the Lord's name in vain (Exodus 20:7). And, two, degrading the sexual union with degusting sexual language. For the latter, the F___ word is most common.

Why are these words added to our language when they do not add to the communication of thoughts? Why are these words primarily expressions that misuse God's name or degrade his creation of the sexual union? Everyone that uses these words knows that they are improper. As a young man, my language was filled with profanity. Yet, when around my parents, I never used these words. Why? I knew that they were dirty, disgusting and sinful. I knew that they were unacceptable around certain people and circumstances. There was no argument about whether these words were foul or not. I chose to fill my talk with foul language. My mouth was not cleansed until I came to Christ as my Lord several years later. The foul talk stopped almost immediately.

We need to be aware that the nature of our words reflects what is in our own hearts. Is it evil or good? We will all be held accountable for what we say on the day of judgment. We may think that swearing is with no ill intent, but we will be held accountable for "every careless word" that we speak.

Either make the tree good and its fruit good, or make the tree bad and its fruit bad, for the tree is known by its fruit. You brood of vipers! **How can you speak good, when you are evil? For out of the abundance of the heart the mouth speaks.** The good person out of his good treasure brings forth good, and the evil person out of his evil treasure brings forth evil. I tell you, **on the day of judgment people will give account for every careless word they speak, for by your words you will be justified, and by your words you will be condemned**. Matthew 12:33-37(ESV)

Our words identify who we are and whom we serve. As Christians, our talk should be wholesome and righteous. There is no place for filthy words coming from a Christian mouth.

From the same mouth come blessing and cursing. My brothers, these things ought not to be so. Does a spring pour forth from the same opening both fresh and salt water? Can a fig tree, my brothers, bear olives, or a grapevine produce figs? Neither can a salt pond yield fresh water. James 3:10-12(ESV)

Sex and our sexual parts are places of privacy. They are only to be exposed within the confines of marriage. Instead, today, sex is exposed at every opportunity. The words that pour forth from our sex driven culture do not build up the sexual union; rather, they degrade the high honor that should be placed on sex between a married man and woman. Sex has been cheapened by our careless and casual use of sexual talk.

> **You must let no unwholesome word come out of your mouth**, but only what is beneficial for the building up of the one in need, that it may give grace to those who hear. And do not grieve the Holy Spirit of God, by whom you were sealed for the day of redemption.
> Ephesians 4:29-30(NET)

God created us with the capacity for humorous joy. But he did not create this beautiful quality to be filled with sexual degradation. Most humor today degrades us as sexual beings. Most jokes are "dirty jokes". Television humor and comedian humor are filled with sexual references. We may laugh, but this is no laughing matter. This misplaced humor will be exposed on the day of judgment, and so will all who find pleasure in it.

> But **sexual immorality and all impurity** or covetousness must not even be named among you, as is proper among saints. **Let there be no filthiness nor foolish talk nor crude joking, which are out of place**, but instead let there be thanksgiving. For you may be sure of this, that **everyone who is sexually immoral or impure**, or who is covetous (that is, an idolater), has no inheritance in the kingdom of Christ and God. Let no one deceive you with empty words, for because of these things the wrath of God comes upon the sons of disobedience. Ephesians 5:3-6(ESV)

Cultural Expectations

Our culture expects teenagers and adults to be having sex outside of marriage. Major department stores have their aisles labeled for condoms.

Of course, a married couple may use condoms, but our teenage students are being encouraged to use condoms when having sex with each other. They are not being told to abstain from sex.

Abortion is encouraged as a means for having sex without having the responsibility for the baby that is created. Most abortions are with unwed mothers (86%). Abortion is as much a promiscuity problem as it is one of murdering an unwanted child.

Sex is an expected mode of advertising. Sexy women are exploited to promote products that have nothing to do with sex. Products to enhance sexual capabilities are openly advertised without reservation. Scanty women's apparel is openly exposed on posters, magazines, billboards and TV ads. There was a day a few decades ago when such exposure was pornographic. Today it is just accepted.

The television and movie industry are filled with sexual exposure, overtones, and humor. Open temptation to sexual sin is an expected aspect of programming and movies. Ratings are given for the degree of exposure (G, PG, PG-13, R and X). The ratings are primarily based on sexual content, filthy language and violence. In other words, they are rated on levels of sinful exposure. And society spends billions of dollars to watch it. It's expected.

All of mankind pays a heavy price for our sexual behavior; far more than the box office receipts. Sexual temptation and sin ruins marriages. It creates millions of children born to mothers without a husband and a father to love and nurture the child. Statistics reveal that broken homes and fatherless homes produce poverty, crime and a host of social problems. All of this could be avoided if sex were honored in our culture.

Christians are to be the salt and light of the world (Matthew 5:13-16). Instead, our culture is filled with darkness. The devil has a foothold with little to no opposition.

Sexually Tempting Dress

Sexually lewd dress is another sexual norm in our culture. We wear what others wear. If others wear miniskirts, we must conform.

If teenage boys are cool if they wear their pants down around their thighs, they wear their pants down around their thighs, even if they have to pull them up every few steps to keep them from falling off.

If tight clothes are in style that reveal just about everything that is under the clothes, that is what is purchased and worn. Even our church pews are filled with women's dress that has the ability to tempt nearly any man. Cleavage has become something to show off. It's stylish, and it's sexually tempting.

We have nearly lost the understanding that God created the body with modest parts that are to be covered up and hidden.

On the contrary, the parts of the body that seem to be weaker are indispensable, **and on those parts of the body that we think less honorable we bestow the greater honor, and our unpresentable parts are treated with greater modesty**, which our more presentable parts do not require. But **God has so composed the body, giving greater honor to the part that lacked it**, 1 Corinthians 12:22-24(ESV)

God created women to have beauty. And he created men to be handsome. But he created the greatest beauty to come from the inner man and woman, not the outer. When we expose the outer parts of our bodies that are to be covered up, we may attract the opposite sex, but our inner beauty has become filthy and unattractive. We have used sexual temptation to get attention.

...likewise also that **women should adorn themselves in respectable apparel, with modesty and self-control**, not with braided hair and gold

71

or pearls or costly attire, but with what is proper for women who profess godliness—with good works. 1 Timothy 2:9-10(ESV)

Sexual Harassment

Our workplaces have become places of sexual harassment. Bosses come on to employees for sexual favors. There is uninvited and unwanted sexual touching. Embarrassing sexual comments are made. Illicit sexual emails are sent around the office. Dirty jokes are openly spoken.

Fortunately, many corporations have established clear standards against sexual harassment as a requirement for employment. But it is sad that we must have our employment threatened in order to act with respect for the sexes and for God's beautiful creation.

Reflection questions

Does your language protect and honor the beauty of the sexual union, or does it expose and dishonor what God has created?

Do you tell dirty jokes? Do you listen and laugh when other tell them?

Do you brag about your sexual affairs?

Is your dress sexually respectful?

Are you willing to avoid entertainment with sexual overtones or explicit exposure?

Do you respect the opposite sex in your surroundings by avoiding any sexual advancements, talk or insinuations?

Chapter Eleven

Mixing Power, Control and Anger with Sex

Rape is not a minor problem. Sexual assault statistics reveal that rape has become a plague upon our nation.

- One out of every three women will be raped in her lifetime.[2]
- 1 in 4 girls and 1 in 6 boys will be sexually assaulted by age 18.[3]
- Alcohol may act for the assailant as a disinhibitor, as an excuse following the assault, or as a strategy to reduce victim resistance. At least 45% of rapists were under the influence of alcohol or drugs at the time of the assault.[4]

---

[2] Koss, M.P. & Harvey, M.R., 1991. The Rape Victim New York, London, New Delhi: Sage Publications.
Ullman, S.E. & Knight, R.A., 1992. Fighting Back: Women's Resistance to Rape. Journal of Interpersonal Violence 7 (1) , 31-42
Randall, Melanie and Haskell, Lori, 1995. "Sexual Violence in Women's Lives: Findings from the Women's Safety Project, A Community-Based Survey." Violence Against Women 1 (2): 6-31
[3] Finkelhor, David, et al. "Sexual Abuse in a National Survey of Adult Men and Women: Prevalence, Characteristics, and Risk Factors." 1990
[4] U.S. Department of Justice, 1994. Violence Against Women. Rockville, Maryland: Bureau of Justice Statistics, U.S. Department of Justice.

- 84% of women who are raped know their assailant.[5]

Rape is different from adultery or fornication. In adultery we are stealing the wife of another man. In fornication (sex outside of marriage) we are stealing the virginity of a future wife. Even if she is not a virgin, we are still partaking of what belongs to her future husband. In either case, adultery or fornication, the sexual act is not forceful, but mutual between the woman and the man.

Rape not only steals from the husband or future husband; rape violently takes from the woman. Normally, sex is a willful event between a man and a woman. Rape is not willful on the part of the woman. She receives no pleasure. The experience for her is terrifying and painful. The offense drives deep within her soul, and the wounds are typically felt for the rest of her life, many times crippling her nature and all relationships for decades to come. [Note that we are referring to rape as a woman being overpowered by a man. However, rape can be woman to man, man to man or man to boy. The emotional damage and confusion most likely will be felt in all situations.]

Why would someone rape? How is it possible to receive sexual pleasure under such circumstances? The answer goes far beyond man's need to fulfill his sexual hormonal drives.

- Rape typically reflects deep seated feelings of inadequacy.[6]
- Rape is NOT a sexual act. Rape IS an act of control and domination.
- Rape is a distortion of human sexuality. It is sexuality in the service of nonsexual needs.[7]

---

[5] Kilpatrick, D.G., C.N. Edmunds and A. Seymour. *Rape in America: A Report to the Nation.* (1992) Arlington, VA: National Victim Center.
[6] Groth, A. Nickolas, *Men Who Rape*, Plenum Press, New York, 1979. Pg.186.
[7] Ibid. Pg. 104, 109.

Types of Rape

Power Rape: Sexual Conquest (55%). Sexuality becomes a means of compensating for *underlying feelings of inadequacy* and serves to express issues of mastery, strength, control, authority, identity and capability.

The intent of the power rapist is to assert his competency and validate his masculinity. Sexuality is the test, and his motive is conquest. Frequently, the power rapist denies that the sexual encounter was forced. He needs to believe the victim wanted and enjoyed it.[8]

Anger Rape (40%): *Expressing and discharging feelings of pent-up anger and rage.* The assault is characterized by physical brutality. Far more actual force is used in the commission of the offense than would be necessary if the intent were simply to overpower the victim and achieve penetration.

The rape experience for this type of offender is one of conscious anger and rage, and he expresses his fury both physically and verbally. *Sex is this man's weapon and rape constitutes the ultimate expression of his anger. Sex is a weapon to defile, degrade and humiliate the victim.*[9]

Sadistic Rape (5%): Fusion of sexuality and aggression. The offender finds the intentional maltreatment of his victim intensely gratifying and takes pleasure in her torment, anguish, distress, helplessness, and suffering.

For these men *the rape experience is one of intense and mounting excitement.* The rapist may find the victim's struggling with him an exciting and erotic experience. Excitement is associated with the inflicting of pain upon his victim. *Hatred and control are eroticized*, and he finds satisfaction in abusing, degrading, humiliating and, in some cases, destroying his captive. His intent is to abuse and torture. *His instrument is sex; his motive is punishment and destruction.*[10]

---

[8] Ibid. Pg. 25, 26, 58.
[9] Ibid. Pg. 13,14,58.
[10] Ibid. Pg. 44, 58.

Old Testament Rape

Adultery, fornication and rape are not new to this time in history. God gave specific commands and punishments for willful acts of sex outside of marriage. Marriage and sex were not to be compromised. The punishments set forth by God were much more severe than the punishments today.

"When a man is discovered lying with a married woman, they shall both die; the woman as well as the man who lay with her; you shall rid Israel of this wickedness. When a virgin is pledged marriage to a man and another man comes upon her in the town and lies with her, you shall bring both of them out to the gate of the town and stone them to death; the girl, because, although in the town, she did not cry for help, and the man because he dishonored another man's wife; you shall rid yourselves of this wickedness. If the man comes upon such a girl in the country and rapes her, then the man alone shall die because he lay with her. You shall do nothing to the girl, she has done nothing worthy of death; this deed is like that of a man who attacks another and murders him, for the man came upon her in the country, and though the girl cried for help, there was no one to rescue her. When a man comes upon a virgin who is not pledged in marriage and forces her to lie with him, and they are discovered, then the man who lies with her shall give the girl's father fifty pieces of silver, and she shall be his wife because he has dishonored her. He is not free to divorce her all his life long." -Deuteronomy 22: 23-29(NIV)

Tamar's rape by her half brother Amon:

Now David's son Absalom had a beautiful sister named Tamar. In the course of time David's son Amnon **fell madly in love with her**. But Amnon became frustrated because he was so **lovesick** over his sister

Tamar. For she was a virgin, and to Amnon it seemed out of the question to do anything to her.

Now Amnon had a friend named Jonadab, the son of David's brother Shimeah. Jonadab was a very crafty man. He asked Amnon, "Why are you, the king's son, so depressed every morning? Can't you tell me?" So Amnon said to him, "I'm in love with Tamar the sister of my brother Absalom." Jonadab replied to him, "Lie down on your bed and pretend to be sick. When your father comes in to see you, say to him, 'Please let my sister Tamar come in so she can fix some food for me. Let her prepare the food in my sight so I can watch. Then I will eat from her hand.'"

So Amnon lay down and pretended to be sick. When the king came in to see him, Amnon said to the king, "Please let my sister Tamar come in so she can make a couple of cakes in my sight. Then I will eat from her hand."

So David sent Tamar to the house saying, "Please go to the house of Amnon your brother and prepare some food for him." So Tamar went to the house of Amnon her brother, who was lying down. She took the dough, kneaded it, made some cakes while he watched, and baked them. But when she took the pan and set it before him, he refused to eat. Instead Amnon said, "Get everyone out of here!" So everyone left.

Then Amnon said to Tamar, "Bring the cakes into the bedroom; then I will eat from your hand." So Tamar took the cakes that she had prepared and brought them to her brother Amnon in the bedroom. As she brought them to him to eat, **he grabbed her and said to her, "Come on! Get in bed with me, my sister!"**

But she said to him, "No, my brother! **Don't humiliate me!** This just isn't done in Israel! Don't do this foolish thing**! How could I ever be rid of my humiliation?** And you would be considered one of the fools in Israel! Just speak to the king, for he will not withhold me from you."

But he refused to listen to her. He overpowered her and humiliated her by raping her. Then Amnon greatly despised her. His disdain toward her surpassed the love he had previously felt toward her. Amnon said to her, "Get up and leave!"

But she said to him, "No I won't, for sending me away now would be worse than what you did to me earlier!" But he refused to listen to her. He called his personal attendant and said to him, "Take this woman out of my sight and lock the door behind her!" (Now she was wearing a long robe, for this is what the king's virgin daughters used to wear.) So Amnon's attendant removed her and bolted the door behind her. Then Tamar put ashes on her head and tore the long robe she was wearing. She put her hands on her head and went on her way, wailing as she went. 2 Samuel 13:1-19(NET)

Did Amnon truly love his half sister Tamar? He could have married her; why didn't he? Why did he think he loved her before the rape, and then he hated her after the rape? Why did he send her away if he loved her? What was Tamar's final state?

Amnon was fooled by his own heart. He thought he loved Tamar, but his motives were completely self-fulfilling. True love is selfless. True love sacrifices something of our lives so that someone else will be blessed. Amnon was out to satisfy his own desires. To truly love Tamar he would have done what was best for her. Instead, he plotted, deceived and forced her. She begged him not to rape her, but he intentionally violated her will. Afterwards, he still could have loved her by marrying her to save her from shame, but he refused to even listen to her plea. He selfishly left her in shame after forcefully taking her virginity from her. Amnon never loved her; he only thought he did. He deceived even himself. He confused love with his own selfish emotions for Tamar. True love is sacrificial, but all of Amnon's emotions and actions were only for self gratification—totally selfish and self centered. After his abusive actions and his own sexual pleasures, his feelings turned to hate. Amnon never truly understood himself. He thought he loved, but in truth he was a very sick and selfish man, whose only concern was to fulfill his own perverted desires. For the rest of her life Tamar paid the heavy price of shame and the loss of her virginity caused by Amnon's actions. Amnon's feeling went from what he thought was love to feelings of hatred. In a sick and perverted way, he probably thought that Tamar would enjoy his forceful attack upon her. Instead, she felt violated by him, and his feelings turned to hate.

The Rapist Is in Need of Serious Spiritual Deliverance

Rape has deep spiritual roots that live within the heart of man. Rape is a serious crime and offense, but the deliverance for the rapist is not shame and punishment. Rape comes out of a wounded, distorted and troubled heart. Jesus was challenged because he mingled with and accepted the lowly sinners of the day. But Jesus replied,

> **It is not the healthy who need a doctor, but the sick.** But go and learn what this means: 'I desire mercy, not sacrifice.' For I have not come to call the righteous, but sinners. Matthew 9:12-13(NIV)

We all suffer from spiritual heart disease. We need the Great Physician to perform heart surgery on each one of us. This is the real answer for the rapist. This is the real answer for all of us.

> The LORD your God will circumcise your hearts and the hearts of your descendants, so that you may love him with all your heart and with all your soul, and live. Deuteronomy 30:6(NIV)

Anger is a powerful drive that lives within man. Anger in itself is not sin, but many of us become angry because of selfishness, and many of us act out our anger by sinning against others. We are commanded not to sin in our anger. We are commanded to search out our own hearts so that we can begin to deal with the root of our problems, which begin in the heart.

In your anger do not sin; when you are on your beds, search your hearts and be silent. Psalm 4:4(NIV)

Rape is a very serious sin against someone else, but the rapist must realize that the first victim is not the one he rapes; the first victim is himself. Deep rooted anger can destroy a person and those around him. Giving into anger gives the devil a foothold, and eventually he will gain the victory by destroying lives. He already has a place in the heart of the rapist.

"In your anger do not sin": Do not let the sun go down while you are still angry, and **do not give the devil a foothold**. Ephesians 4:26-27(NIV)

There is a great hope. Jesus came to destroy the devil's work. He is our healer, our protector, our strength and our deliverer. He has given to us his very own Spirit to live within us to give us the victory over sinful temptations and the devil. He has given to us his power to practice his love rather than our selfishness.

Dear children, do not let anyone lead you astray. He who does what is right is righteous, just as he is righteous. **He who does what is sinful is of the devil, because the devil has been sinning from the beginning. The reason the Son of God appeared was to destroy the devil's work**. No one who is born of God will continue to sin, because God's seed remains in him; he cannot go on sinning, because he has been born of God. This is how we know who the children of God are and who the children of the devil are: Anyone who does not do what is right is not a child of God; nor is anyone who does not love his brother. 1 John 3:7-10(NIV)

We are responsible for our own anger and our angry actions. We are to "get rid of all moral filth" that comes about from our own anger.

My dear brothers, take note of this: Everyone should be quick to listen, slow to speak and slow to become angry, for **man's anger does not bring about the righteous life that God desires**. Therefore, **get rid of all moral filth** and the evil that is so prevalent and humbly accept the word planted in you, which can save you. James 1:19-21(NIV)

Out of the Heart

Anger comes out of the heart. Sexual immorality also comes out of the heart. Rape is a heart issue; it comes out of the heart.

The good man brings good things out of the good stored up in his heart, and **the evil man brings evil things out of the evil stored up in his heart**. For out of the overflow of his heart his mouth speaks. Luke 6:45(NIV)

For **out of the heart come evil thoughts**, murder, **adultery, sexual immorality**, theft, false testimony, slander. Matthew 15:19(NIV)

What could possibly go wrong in the heart to cause a man to forcefully have sex? Hatred? Bitterness? Insecurity? Feeling rejection? Feeling out of control? Deep wounds from emotional and physical abuse?

Only through Jesus Christ is the heart of man healed and changed.

Reflection questions

How does your inner suffering affect your sexual outlook?

How does anger and aggression enter into your sexual drive?

How have you ever coerced a woman to have sex beyond her will?

Have you ever felt guilty about your sexual activity?

Does your drive to have sex control you? Have you ever been out of control?

Do you need help in this area?

Chapter Twelve

Sexual Abuse to Men and Boys

We normally think of sexual abuse as happening to girls and women, not to boys and men. This is a hidden misconception. Men and boys are frequent victims of sexual abuse.

- One in four women and one in six men will be sexually assaulted in their lifetime. [11]
- One in four victims of sexual assault under the age of twelve is a boy.[12]
- 92,700 men are forcibly raped each year in the United States.[13]

God created sex as a union between a married man and woman. The devil's aim is to destroy every life-giving aspect of his creation. He perverts, lies and distorts in order to destroy and rob us of life. Jesus calls the devil a thief who comes to steal and kill and destroy.

---

[11] Finkelhor, David, et al. *Sexual Abuse in a National Survey of Adult Men and Women: Prevalence, Characteristics and Risk Factors.* Child Abuse and Neglect: The International Journal v 14 n1 p 19-28, 1990.

[12] *Sexual Assault of Young Children as Reported to Law Enforcement: Victim, Incident, and Offender Characteristics.* US Department of Justice Statistics.

[13] Tjaden, Patricia and Nancy Thoennes. *Prevalence, Incidence, and Consequences of Violence Against Women: Findings from the National Violence Against Women Survey.* National Institute of Justice, US Department of Justice, November 1998.

The thief comes only to steal and kill and destroy; I have come that they may have life, and have it to the full. John 10:10(NIV)

Marriage and the sexual union is one of God's most beautiful creations. It gives us a picture of the marriage of the Church to Jesus. It is the place where we come to know the love of our heavenly Father through the love of our earthly father. It is the place where children are born, loved, cared for and taught about God and his ways. The family, a creation of God, is the foundation of every nation. If Satan can pervert and destroy the family structure as God created it to be, he can destroy the Church and the nations.

Sexual perversions of every kind give the devil great delight, for this is key to his ultimate battle plan against God's kingdom, to destroy the foundations of the family. He works on many fronts, which we have already discussed. Sexual abuse to men and boys is part of his destruction plan. Sexually abused boys become wounded husbands and fathers. In their wounds, they can become weakened and even abusive to their own children.

Jesus spoke plainly about the high value that God puts on a child. He also spoke quite strongly about the seriousness of those who cause little children to sin.

At that time the disciples came to Jesus and asked, "Who is the greatest in the kingdom of heaven?"

He called a little child and had him stand among them. And he said: "I tell you the truth, unless you change and become like little children, you will never enter the kingdom of heaven. Therefore, whoever humbles himself like this child is the greatest in the kingdom of heaven.

"And whoever welcomes a little child like this in my name welcomes me. **But if anyone causes one of these little ones who believe in me to sin, it would be better for him to have a large**

millstone hung around his neck and to be drowned in the depths of the sea. Matthew 18:1-6(NIV)

Children are the next generation, and they are the ones through whom God will create the next generation. He holds every father responsible to treat their children with love and to bring them up in a godly manner. Terribly, fathers have fallen far short of their godly calling. In fact, many have abused their children in many ways, and many fathers are the victims of abuse themselves.

What Are the Consequences of Sexual Abuse to Boys?

Most of the time the sexual abuse is by someone the child knows and may be a close person who is supposed to be trusted as someone who loves him and someone who is in authority, such as a father, mother, stepparent, uncle, neighbor, spiritual leader, camp counselor or any other trusted close relationship. This causes great confusion for the little boy who is not old enough and wise enough to fully understand what is happening to him. He is truly a victim—not just to his body, but to his entire spiritual makeup.

Little children look up to the adults in their lives for identity, understanding, reality and direction. Children come into this life with no preconceived understanding or knowledge. What they accept as true and normal comes from their environment. If they are given a lie, they accept the lie without question. Lies bring about destruction. Life comes from the truth. Jesus said,

"If you hold to my teaching, you are really my disciples. Then you will know the truth, and **the truth will set you free**." John 8:31-32(NIV)

God created sex to be isolated between a married man and woman. When a little boy or adolescent is overwhelmed to have sex by an authoritative adult, he is being told that this is normal, which is a lie. His identity with a true man is replaced with identity with a perverted male or female. He becomes confused. His inner conscience, as given to him by God, does not agree with what is happening to him. He may not want the affair, but he does not feel like he can control it. Now he is trapped within himself with no place to turn when the perpetrator comes again. His body may respond to the sexual advancement with sexual sensation—even climax. Now the boy is really confused. He does not want the advancement, but his body is responding to its pleasure. This brings on guilt and more confusion. And as he grows up, he may develop all sorts of crippling behaviors as a consequence.

- Guilt
- Anxiety
- Depression
- Interpersonal Isolation
- Shame
- Low Self-esteem
- Self-destructive Behavior
- Post-traumatic Stress Reactions
- Poor Body Imagery
- Sleep Disturbances
- Anorexia or Bulimia
- Addictive Behaviors: (Alcoholism, Drug Addiction, Gambling, Overeating, Overspending, Sexual Obsession or Compulsion)
- Relational and/or Sexual Dysfunction
- Confusion Over Sexual Identity

If he was sexually abused by a woman, maybe his mother, when he is older, his view of women may become distorted. He will likely have a distorted understanding of true motherly love—nurturing, caring, protecting and honoring his father. He may develop an inner distrust of women. This may drive him to be a powerful controller in his relationships with women, especially his wife and daughters. This can be driven by fear to trust a woman and anger towards women. It can damage his future marriage and family relationships. This happens all because of unwanted sexual abuse by a woman who should have loved him. Instead, she took advantage of him to fulfill her own unmet needs and passed it off as love for him. What a lie! What confusion for the boy!

If he is sexually abused by a man, he may question his own sexual identity. We may be born as a male with all the right biological features, but we acquire sexual identity. All of us from conception were carried in our mother's womb. At birth, we were mostly held by our mothers, and probably fed by her. Our first identity is with our mothers. As boys, in our early years we transfer our identity to our fathers. This transference is supported by other males—older brothers, uncles, grandfathers and other boys. Our personal makeup may help this transference, such as size and strength, or the driving desire to do boy things, such as wrestle, play in the mud and climb trees. But not all boys are the same. Some are not as tough and strong, but they are just as much male.

What happens to our male identity if another older male sexually advances upon us? They are always bigger and stronger. They are usually in authority over us. And now our identity with this male is sexual. This is one of those lies that Jesus talks about. Remember, he said, "the truth will set you free." Satan is a liar. He began leading man astray with Adam and Eve, and he continues to lead us down a path of destruction with lies that we believe. Jesus spoke of the devil as a liar.

> He was a murderer from the beginning, not holding to the truth, for there is no truth in him. When he lies, he speaks his native language, for he is a liar and the father of lies. John 8:44(NIV)

When a boy is sexually abused by a man, Satan uses this occurrence to lie to the boy about male identity and character. This lie can destroy his entire life because he does not see himself as who he was truly created by the hand of God. In truth, his sexual orientation before and after the assaults is the same, and did not change by the assaults. However, a lie is planted that may not ever be exposed for the rest of his life. He may go through life questioning his masculinity or his sexual identity. He may go through life feeling inherently weak, inadequate and powerless over his life. All of this is because he has been lied to through the sinful and unwanted behavior of another male.

There is great debate of the causes of homosexuality. But consider that compared to heterosexuals, non-heterosexuals are about two to three times as likely to have experienced childhood sexual abuse.[14]

Reflection questions

How do you see yourself as a man?

Who do you think were the greatest influences upon your view of yourself? What did they instill in you and how?

Were you abused? How does that make you feel about yourself? About men? About women? About fathers? About mothers?

---

[14] Mayer, L. S., M.B., M.S., Ph.D., & McHugh, P. R., M.D. (fall 2015). Sexuality and Gender Findings from the Biological, Psychological, and Social Sciences. *The New Atlantis*, (50), 1-143. Pg. 7. Retrieved August 31, 2016, from http://www.thenewatlantis.com/docLib/20160819_TNA50SexualityandGender.pdf

Chapter Thirteen

Homosexuality

Homosexuality has gotten a lot of attention in the media. All kinds of things are being said. Some are true, and some have no basis. Some claim that homosexuality is a genetic trait that is irreversible. Other experts claim that homosexuality is a sexual identity issue that begins in the first few years of a child's life and can progress toward a homosexual or heterosexual identity depending upon many factors as the child matures.

Some men do not like their homosexual tendencies, but if they believe that they were genetically born that way, there is nothing they can do about it. On the other end of the spectrum of beliefs, there are those who think homosexual attractions are purely a personal choice, and that a person chooses to have same sex attractions. And, if that is true, he can choose not to have these attractions and live a life as a heterosexual. Both extremes are ill-founded and give no hope to the one who is struggling with his sexual identity.

Bias views do not help anyone, and bias does not usually reveal the truth; rather, it closes off our understanding and separates us into opposing groups. So let's take a scientific look at homosexuality and try to answer a few questions: What is its prevalence? What causes homosexuality? Can a homosexual become heterosexual? And, what does the Bible say about homosexuality and other sexually practices?

Prevalence of Homosexuality

A 2015 Gallup Poll revealed that Americans perceive that about 23% of our population is homosexual, which is a gross overestimate. Gallup surveyed individuals across America asking "Do you, personally, identify as lesbian, gay, bisexual or transgender?" Out of 58,000 people surveyed, only 3.8% responded affirming their identity in one of these categories.[15] If we are going to find truthful answers to the questions about homosexuality, we must first realize that our culture through the media, government and even corporations are indoctrinating our society with impressions and beliefs that are not substantiated.

Jones and Yarhouse have done an exhaustive survey of studies on homosexuality prior to the year 2000, attempting to define the validity of many reports in this area. Regarding prevalence, they concluded similar results to the more recent Gallup Poll.

More recent and more credible studies suggest that less than 3%, and perhaps less than 2%, of males are homosexually active in a given year.

Female homosexuality is estimated at approximately half or less than the male rates and appears to characterize less than 2% of the female population.[16]

The National Center for Health Statistics surveyed 34,557 adults aged 18 and over in 2013. There results were similar, finding that less than 2.3% identified as gay, lesbian or bisexual.

---

[15] Newport, Frank. "Americans Greatly Overestimate Percent Gay, Lesbian in U.S."*Gallup.com*. N.p., 21 May 2015. Web. 12 Aug. 2016.

[16] Jones, Stanton L., and Mark A. Yarhouse. *Homosexuality: The Use of Scientific Research in the Church's Moral Debate*. Downers Grove, IL: InterVarsity, 2000. Print. Pg. 46.

Among all U.S. adults aged 18 and over, 96.6% identified as straight, 1.6% identified as gay or lesbian, and 0.7% identified as bisexual. The remaining 1.1% of adults identified as "something else" (0.2%), selected "I don't know the answer" (0.4%), or refused to provide an answer (0.6%).[17]

What Causes Homosexuality?

There appears to be several bias views as to the cause. There are three extremes. One, that it is genetically derived such that a person is born as a homosexual or heterosexual, so there is no opportunity to change. A second view concludes that sexual orientation is initiated in the early years of life and progresses in stages during maturation.

These factors can be complex, and cannot be simplified into a list. Relationships with their father and mother, the relationship between their father and mother, the temperaments of their father and mother and the child's own natural temperaments can all play a part in a child's development of his views of himself, relationships and life in general. In summary, this view concludes that our sexual identity is environmentally derived.

And the third position is that becoming homosexual is a personal choice. Temptations may have presented themselves through other independent means, but in the end, each person decides his sexual identity for himself.

These are the three extremes, genetically derived, experientially derived and decisively derived. So, is there clear-cut evidence to substantiate one of these positions over another? Again, Jones and Yarhouse have taken a scientific look at the preponderance of data available as of 2000.

---

[17] Ward BW, Dahlhamer JM, Galinsky AM, Joestl SS. Sexual orientation and health among U.S. adults: National Health Interview Survey, 2013. National health statistics reports; no 77. Hyattsville, MD: National Center for Health Statistics. 2014., http://www.cdc.gov/nchs/data/nhsr/nhsr077.pdf

For those who are trying to gather information from science on the origins of homosexuality, we would conclude that no research to date provides ample support for any one theory to the exclusion of another. Let us be clear about what we are saying and not saying: we are not saying that the biological theories have been disproven. We are not saying that the psychological theories have been proven. Neither are we urging cynical attitudes toward the hard work of science; we have made tremendous advances in our understanding of persons and how we function, but the jury is still out on these complicated questions of causation. *We are saying that the scientific evidence about causation is simply inconclusive at this time.*[18]

In other words, the scientific studies do not conclude that the sole cause is genetic; neither do they conclude that the sole cause is socially induced. Instead, they conclude that it is likely driven by a host of factors, including genetics, social factors and personal choices.

Further, readers must understand that we may not have to choose between particular theories with the nature or nurture clusters, between nature and nurture as general categories, or even between nature, nurture and human freedom. It may be more accurate and more helpful to pursue an "interactionist hypothesis" where **various psychological, environmental and biological factors, together with human choice, contribute to different degrees that vary from person to person**.

Based on our understanding of the present research, we are both inclined to embrace a "weighted interactionist hypothesis."[19]

---

[18] Jones, Stanton L., and Mark A. Yarhouse. *Homosexuality: The Use of Scientific Research in the Church's Moral Debate*. Downers Grove, IL: InterVarsity, 2000. Print. Pg. 46.
[19] Ibid.

Many experts in this area agree that an "interactionist hypothesis" is probably the best explanation for the origins of same-sex attraction.[20]

In other words, they conclude that it is not one cause, but a combination of causes, all contributing to our sexual identity—homosexual or heterosexual.

Note that all of these factors can work together to influence our sexual identity. Also note that we are all born with our own temperaments, which are genetically derived. These temperaments are not specifically sexual in nature, but when combined with environmental factors and personal choices they can play a part in our sexual identity.

In summary, it is conceivable how there may be genetic factors that can make some people more vulnerable to becoming homosexual when several other environmental factors are also present in one's life. Keep in mind that these are not sexual genes, but, rather personality traits that can exist for anyone, male or female, heterosexual or homosexual. These factors, genetic or environmental, do not guarantee to produce homosexuality, and personal choice to pursue this sexual orientation is also a pivotal factor. So we have genetics, environment and personal choice. All three must coincide in order for a homosexual identity to manifest.

There have been many studies over many decades. And, many of these studies were incomplete, cursory, biased, or not very scientifically structured. None the less, several have reviewed these studies and given their assessments, as Jones and Yarhouse who were just quoted.

The National Association of Reparative Therapy (NARTH) did another independent review of the studies available over many years with a similar conclusion.

As members of NARTH's Scientific Advisory Committee, we feel obligated to inform both the scientific and lay communities about the plethora of studies that lead to a singular conclusion: *Homosexuality is*

---

[20] Ibid., Pg. 91.

not innate, immutable, or without significant risk to medical, psychological, and relational health.

We wrote a reasonably comprehensive, historical review of more than 100 years of clinical and research literature.[21]

They found no data confirming an exclusive genetic cause for homosexuality. They also found no data confirming that those with same-sex attractions cannot be replaced with heterosexual attractions.

A more recent (2015) exhaustive study by The New Atlantis, A Journal of Technology and Society, made similar conclusions.[22]

---

[21] Phelan, J. E., Whitehead, N., & Sutton, P. M. (2009). What Research Shows: NARTH's Response to the APA Claims on Homosexuality. A Report of the Scientific Advisory Committee of the National Association for Research and Therapy of Homosexuality. *JOURNAL OF HUMAN SEXUALITY, 1*. Retrieved August 31, 2016, from http://www.peoplecanchange.com/change/whatresearchshowsnarth.pdf

[22] Paul R. McHugh, M.D. requested Lawrence S. Mayer, M.B., M.S., Ph.D. to analyze the data to date on homosexuality. Dr. Mayer states: I am a biostatistician and epidemiologist who focuses on the design, analysis, and interpretation of experimental and observational data in public health and medicine, particularly when the data are complex in terms of underlying scientific issues. I am a research physician, having trained in medicine and psychiatry in the U.K. and received the British equivalent (M.B.) to the American M.D.

It [this report] arose from a request from Paul R. McHugh, M.D., the former chief of psychiatry at Johns Hopkins Hospital and one of the leading psychiatrists in the world. Dr. McHugh requested that I review a monograph he and colleagues had drafted on subjects related to sexual orientation and identity; my original assignment was to guarantee the accuracy of statistical inferences and to review additional sources. In the months that followed, I closely read over five hundred scientific articles on these topics and perused hundreds more.

Part One: Sexual Orientation

• The understanding of sexual orientation as an innate, biologically fixed property of human beings—the idea that people are "born that way"—is not supported by scientific evidence.

• While there is evidence that biological factors such as genes and hormones are associated with sexual behaviors and attractions, there are no compelling causal biological explanations for human sexual orientation. While minor differences in the brain structures and brain activity between homosexual and heterosexual individuals have been identified by researchers, such neurobiological findings do not demonstrate whether these differences are innate or are the result of environmental and psychological factors.

• Longitudinal studies of adolescents suggest that sexual orientation may be quite fluid over the life course for some people, with one study estimating that as many as 80% of male adolescents who report same-sex attractions no longer do so as adults (although the extent to which this figure reflects actual changes in same-sex attractions and not just artifacts of the survey process has been contested by some researchers).

• Compared to heterosexuals, non-heterosexuals are about two to three times as likely to have experienced childhood sexual abuse.[23]

Part Three: Gender Identity

• The hypothesis that gender identity is an innate, fixed property of human beings that is independent of biological sex—that a person might be "a man trapped in a woman's body" or "a woman trapped in a man's body"—is not supported by scientific evidence.

---

[23] Mayer, L. S., M.B., M.S., Ph.D., & McHugh, P. R., M.D. (fall 2015). Sexuality and Gender Findings from the Biological, Psychological, and Social Sciences. *The New Atlantis,* (50), 1-143. Pg. 7. Retrieved August 31, 2016, from http://www.thenewatlantis.com/docLib/20160819_TNA50SexualityandGender.pdf

- According to a recent estimate, about 0.6% of U.S. adults identify as a gender that does not correspond to their biological sex.
- Studies comparing the brain structures of transgender and non-transgender individuals have demonstrated weak correlations between brain structure and cross-gender identification. These correlations do not provide any evidence for a neurobiological basis for cross-gender identification.[24]

Sexual Identity

Biologically, we are all born as men or women. Our sexual features and organs are very evident. Other features, such as facial hair, tone of voice, bone structure, muscle mass, and other physical indicators are quite obvious. We are born with a biological sexual identity, but, then, we must acquire a mental and emotional sexual identity. The two, biological and mental/emotional, normally match, but for a few percent of the population, these identities do not match.

As already discussed, scientific studies **do not** agree that this mismatch is genetically determined. Genetic character traits may have an influence, but early relational factor and personal choices must also be present for someone to have a mismatch between his biological identity and his mental and emotional identity. Let's look at a few scenarios to visualize how this may happen.

Every man is born with a close identity with his mother. He spends nine months in her womb. Immediately after birth he is held close to his mother and is fed in her arms. She is the one who comforts him, baths his naked body, changes his poopy pants and cleans off his sexual parts. She is the one he is most close to from the time he is born until he is one, two or three years old. During this early time the normal progression is for boys to leave their identity with their mother and form an identity with their father. This is how God designed it.

---

[24] Ibid. Pg. 8.

Typically, a boy has a masculine temperament and physical structure. He sees his father and he is drawn to him. He sees himself much like his father and other males. More importantly, the father is drawn to his son. He plays with him rough. He invites him to do what he does, like sit on his lap on the riding lawnmower, play catch, wrestle, build things together, work together, go fishing and many other activities that mostly men and boys do. Unaware, the young boy looks at his mother, he looks at his father and he looks at himself. He makes a choice to identify. If his father is loving and masculine and he pursues his son, and the son will naturally identify with his father.

If the father is not loving and masculine, and if the mother is the dominant leader of the family, the boy may be confused. In addition, if the boy is not husky, but frail, and if he likes to be in the house reading or playing the piano while his husky older brothers are out running around with Dad, this may reinforce his identity with his mom and he may not acquire an identity with Dad.

Physical, emotional and/or sexual abuse by the father may drive him away from identifying with his father. As previously stated, homosexuals are two to three times more likely to have experienced childhood sexual abuse. Homosexuality is an identity issue. It can be complex with many possibilities that can influence a heterosexual or homosexual identity. This identity transition from the mother to the father occurs in the early years. Most of us cannot remember much before we were five years old, and by this time the identity choice likely has already taken root. That may be why most homosexuals think they were born that way, because the choice was determined at a very early age—but it was an unconscious choice.

Where does choice play a part? Certainly, a two or three years old does not make a rational choice to identify himself as homosexual and to engage in homosexual activities. These choices come later in the formative years or even later. As previously quoted by Mayer and McHugh from *The New Atlantis*, "Longitudinal studies of adolescents suggest that sexual orientation may be quite fluid over the life course for some people, with one study estimating that as many as 80% of male adolescents who report same-sex attractions no longer do so as adults."

Understanding what happened in a boy's life, and then working to acquire an identity that matches his physical identity is the secret to forming a heterosexual identity.

Can a Homosexual Become Heterosexual?

This becomes a very difficult question to answer because it is very difficult to measure and define the transition. For example, if a homosexual marries and exclusively has heterosexual relations with his wife, does that mean that he is now heterosexual? What if he still has homosexual desires, even if not practiced? What if his homosexual desires are infrequent? What infrequency is necessary to define him as heterosexual? Does it need to be zero? What if he is bisexual? Is he both a homosexual and a heterosexual? What if he predominantly has heterosexual relationships, but then infrequently has a homosexual encounter, say once every few years?

I think we would all agree that a successful transformation occurred if a homosexual transitioned to heterosexual by never again having a homosexual temptation or interaction. But, again, how do we define "never"? "Never" would have to mean the rest of one's life. What if he only lived a few years and then died? Would we be convinced? I think we would be convinced if the transition occurred in his twenties or thirties and then in his nineties he still proclaimed that he was temptation free. But we would have to survey these converts over fifty, sixty or seventy years to get the data, and then, maybe a hundred years from now we would have an answer.

I think a better question is, can a homosexual lead a satisfying heterosexual married life—become a loving husband and father such that homosexual desires are minimal and do not interfere with his heterosexual marriage and resulting family?

And if he never married, success may be defined as never practicing homosexuality and rarely, if ever, tempted to do so, but at the same time he finds himself attracted by the opposite sex. Another measure for a non-practicing homosexual would be his level of contentment, joy, his functional and prosperous life and his self-worth and esteem. Again, how do we measure these attributes? And consider that many heterosexuals do not rate highly in these areas.

For the most part, heterosexual men are not tempted to have homosexual fantasies or relationships. However, this may not be the case for someone who has previously lived out homosexual fantasies or relationships. He may have a successful, happy, satisfying and prosperous heterosexual relationship, and still struggle with his former temptations. The key to defining a successful transition should not be limited to sexual arousal. It should be defined in terms of the prosperity of his overall life as a heterosexual, especially his marriage and family, if he is married.

Our lives are much greater than our sexual practices. When someone's sexual identity becomes the main focus of his life, it should be obvious that there is a consuming unhealthy identity crisis.

Matt Moore is a Christian writer who has an inspiring blog and following. Here are a few initial paragraphs of his July 31, 2016 blog, *I am not Homosexual . . . or Heterosexual or Bisexual or Any-Other-Kind-Of-Sexual*

I'm often asked why I don't use the terms "gay" or "homosexual" to describe myself—or even "bisexual" now that I've begun to dip my toes in the "heterosexual" dating world. If throwing quotations around these terms doesn't insinuate strongly enough my distaste for them, let me say it plainly: I am not a fan of the prevalent language used in our society to think and talk about human sexuality. I believe it is pregnant with faulty ideas that skew a person's self-perspective and hinder Christian growth. I refuse to submit myself to it by identifying as homosexual or heterosexual or bisexual or asexual or any-other-kind-of-sexual.

Many of my Christian brothers and sisters don't understand this. They see no harm in using self-descriptors like *gay* and *homosexual* to convey that one is attracted to the same gender or self-descriptors like *straight* and *heterosexual* to convey that one is attracted to the opposite gender. They don't understand why I opt to use lengthier descriptions to narrate my experience when I could simply say, "I am gay." Sure, it takes a lot less time to say, "I am gay," than it does to say, "I am a fallen human being who is riddled with sin and who experiences all kinds of inclinations that seek to entice me away from God's good design, including a sinful sexual attraction toward the same gender." The latter is a mouthful! However, I find it to be a necessary mouthful—for a couple of significant reasons.

First, I believe the sexuality language of our day flows from an ideology that gives sexuality a higher seat at the "identity table" than I think it should. These labels are not just words used to describe a person's inclinations, preferences, or behaviors—these labels are loaded with ideas about *who a person is*. In our current context, someone's sexuality largely dictates who their friends are, the bars they frequent, the country clubs they join, the bumper stickers they put on their cars, and the kind of flag they wave. Before I converted to Christianity, my attraction to men was the chief informer of my self-perspective. I didn't see Matt Moore as just a man; I saw Matt Moore as a gay man. Every person I knew in the LGBT community viewed and described themselves in the same way. Above so many other things, *we were gay*.

I feel like if I were to again label myself as "gay", I would be embracing the idea that my [broken] sexuality is a defining mark of who I am as a person. And I don't want to operate in a mentality in which my sexual desires have identity-shaping power in my life. I don't want the way I perceive and put language to my experiences to be an open door through which a false identity marker can slip in and begin to overshadow my truest identity marker: my position in Jesus. I am primarily the righteousness of God in Christ—not my jacked up sexuality. When God causes an imperishable body to swallow up this sin-corrupted flesh I presently dwell in, my attraction to men will be no more. I will not carry my broken sexuality with me into glory. Therefore, I refuse to view or name it as a part of *who I am* today.[25]

So we might define a successful transition as one who has found his true identity outside of, or other than, a sexual identity label.

Homosexuality or heterosexuality is not just a biological outcome, like getting hungry when we have not eaten for several hours. Granted, we all have sexual hormones, but the hormones are not homosexual or heterosexual—they are just sexual. The drive to have homosexual or heterosexual relationships are driven by our identities. Sex is not just for sexual gratification; it is a relationship. Relationships are a part of our spiritual makeup. We are all biological and spiritual beings. We all have a body and a soul. Scripture is clear about that. (Matthew 10:28, 1 Thessalonians 5:23, Genesis 2:7) Our identity is a part of our soul, and according to Dr. Joseph Nicolosi, it is highly influenced by family relationships. Dr. Nicolosi is one of three founding members–and former President–of the National Association for Research and Therapy of Homosexuality (NARTH), a 1,000-member professional association founded in 1992. Dr. Nicolosi states that homosexuality is a development, not solely a biological genetic outcome.

Homosexuality is a developmental problem that is almost always the result of problems in family relation, particularly between father and

---

[25] For the full blog transcript: I am not Homosexual…or Heterosexual or Bisexual or Any-Other-Kind-Of-Sexual. (2016). Retrieved August 15, 2016, from http://www.moorematt.org/i-am-not-homosexual-or-heterosexual-or-bisexual-or-any-other-kind-of-sexual/

son. As a result of failure with father, the boy does not fully internalize male gender-identity, and develops homosexuality.[26]

Dr. Nicolosi has dedicated his life to reparative therapy for men who desire to "reduce their unwanted same-sex attractions".

For many years, I have been assisting men and women—mostly, persons who are still at a crossroads about their sexual identity—to reduce their same-sex attractions and explore their heterosexual potential.[27]

I have helped many men reduce their unwanted same-sex attractions, so that they lose their compelling, life-disrupting power, and assisted them in exploring and developing their heterosexual potential.[28]

There have been several evaluations of the scientific studies regarding homosexuality. Dr. Nicolosi has the advantage of having worked with men in their struggles—engaging with them in their lives. He has witnessed firsthand what has gone on in their past, how they see themselves and what has led them into a new understanding of themselves. These understandings not only reveal the causes of same sex attraction, they also begin to bring understanding for what is missing and must be part of reducing homosexual attractions and increasing heterosexual attractions.

Dr. Nicolosi describes what he sees as the root cause of most homosexual attractions.

In infancy, both boys and girls are emotionally attached to the mother. In psychodynamic language, mother is the first love object. She meets all her child's primary needs. Girls can continue to develop

---

[26] Nicolosi, Joseph. *Reparative Therapy of Male Homosexuality: A New Clinical Approach*. Northvale, NJ: J. Aronson, 1991. Print. pg. 25

[27] Home. (n.d.). Retrieved August 27, 2016, from http://www.josephnicolosi.com/

[28] Ibid.

in their feminine identification through the relationship with their mothers. On the other hand, a boy has an additional developmental task—to disidentify from his mother and identify with his father.

While learning language ("he and she," "his and hers"), the child discovers that the world is divided into natural opposites of boys and girls, men and women. At this point, a little boy will not only begin to observe the difference, but also he must now decide where he himself fits in this gender-divided world.[29]

Dr. Niclolosi goes on to emphasize that this identity transformation is highly affected by the young son's relationship with his father.

Tragically, it is an all-too-familiar pattern. In fifteen years, I have spoken with hundreds of homosexual men. Perhaps there are exceptions, but I have never met a single homosexual man who said he had a close, loving, and respectful relationship with his father.

I have found this to be a good test of the early father-son bond; who does the little boy run to when he is happy, proud of something he has done, looking for encouragement, or seeking fun and excitement? If it is always Mom, then something is wrong with the father-son relationship.

In our own clinical work, and from the experience of the many men we have known, it seems very rare for a man who struggles with homosexuality to feel that he was sufficiently loved affirmed, and mentored by his father while growing up or to feel that he identified with his father as a male role model. In fact, often the son remembers the relationship as characterized by a felling of neglect, mutual hostility, and paternal lack of interest (a form of psychological abandonment).[30]

---

[29] Nicolosi, J., & Nicolosi, L. A. (2002). *A parent's guide to preventing homosexuality*. Downers Grove, IL: InterVarsity Press. pg. 23.

[30] Ibid. pg. 31.

Every boy has a deep longing to be held, to be loved by a father figure, to be mentored into the world of men, and to have his masculine nature affirmed and declared good enough by his male peers, his male elders, and mentors. If none of these relationships is strong enough to welcome the boy into the world of men, then he will yearn after other men from a distance. Like Richard Wyler [see note], I have never known a single case of a homosexual man who was not wounded in his relationships within the male world.[31]

[Note: Richard Wyler is founder of People Can Change, (www.peoplecanchange.com). Wyler has had his own life changed from a homosexual identity to a successful and prosperous heterosexual identity and life.]

What are the conclusive inferences from these exhaustive studies? Homosexuality is a sexual identity issue. With proper counseling, sexual identity that matches the biological sex have been established, allowing one to live a normal heterosexual life. Hundreds, if not thousands, of men have successfully established truthful sexual identities and now live out happy and prosperous heterosexual relationships.

Homosexuality has its roots in a misplaced identity. The homosexual is forever searching for what can only be found in a heterosexual relationship, as God created it to be. According to the Family Research Council, "few homosexual relationships achieve the longevity common in marriages". Homosexuals typically do not find contentment in one partner. "Research indicates that the average male homosexual has hundreds of sex partners in his lifetime."[32]

---

[31] Ibid. pg 32.

[32] Dailey, Ph. D, Timothy J. . "Comparing the Lifestyles of Homosexual Couples to Married Couples ." *Family Research Council*. Family Research Council, 04 Mar 2004. Web. 19 Oct 2011. <http://www.frc.org/content/comparing-the-lifestyles-of-homosexual-couples-to-married-couples>.

Do not assume that every homosexual wants to remain a homosexual. Many want help to reduce their homosexual identity and to live out a heterosexual life. As Dr. Niclolosi has stated,

"I have helped many men reduce their unwanted same-sex attractions, so that they lose their compelling, life-disrupting power, and assisted them in exploring and developing their heterosexual potential."[33]

Explore his website for many testimonials.[34] Search the web for even more.

What Does the Bible Say about Homosexuality?

The Bible is not neutral on this issue. Both Old and New Testaments are very clear that homosexual practices are contrary to God's will and become a perversion of his creation.

Do not lie with a man as one lies with a woman; that is detestable. Leviticus 18:22 (NIV)

If a man lies with a man as one lies with a woman, both of them have done what is detestable. They must be put to death; their blood will be on their own heads. Leviticus 20:13 (NIV)

For the wrath of God is revealed from heaven against all ungodliness and unrighteousness of men, who by their unrighteousness suppress the truth. For what can be known about God is plain to them, because God has shown it to them. For his invisible attributes, namely, his eternal power and divine nature, have been

---

[33] Home. (n.d.). Retrieved August 27, 2016, from http://www.josephnicolosi.com/
[34] Client Stories. (n.d.). Retrieved August 27, 2016, from http://www.josephnicolosi.com/

clearly perceived, ever since the creation of the world, in the things that have been made. So they are without excuse. For although they knew God, they did not honor him as God or give thanks to him, but they became futile in their thinking, and their foolish hearts were darkened. Claiming to be wise, they became fools, and exchanged the glory of the immortal God for images resembling mortal man and birds and animals and reptiles.

Therefore God gave them up in the lusts of their hearts to impurity, to the dishonoring of their bodies among themselves, because they exchanged the truth about God for a lie and worshiped and served the creature rather than the Creator, who is blessed forever! Amen.

For this reason God gave them up to dishonorable passions. For their women exchanged natural relations for those that are contrary to nature; and the men likewise gave up natural relations with women and were consumed with passion for one another, men committing shameless acts with men and receiving in themselves the due penalty for their error. Romans 1:18-27(ESV)

These statements from God's word are very strong and pointed, but let's make a clear distinction between temptation and practice. Temptation is not the sin here. Jesus was tempted to sin, but did not sin. (Hebrews 4:15, Matthew 4:1, Luke 4:2, 13) Most heterosexuals also face sexual temptations, but do not have to succumb to sin. A husband may be tempted with sexual arousal with a woman other than his wife, but he does not have to succumb to having an adulterous affair. Jesus equates lust from our heart for another woman to adultery. (Matthew 5:28) Pornography is promoted as the temptation to lust for another woman. The temptation is not the sin; subjecting our eyes to pornography for sexual pleasure is the sin. And, a single man will most likely be tempted to have a sexual relationship, but does not have a wife to satisfy his sexual drives. He keeps himself pure by choosing not to engage in sexual practices, even though he is tempted to do so.

In like manner, God's wrath is not against someone who has a misplaced sexual identity, through no fault of his own. His wrath is against those who oppose and "suppress the truth" through their own wicked hearts and schemes. These are the rebellious against God.

And even when we fall to our temptations we can come clean through our confessions of wrongdoing.

If we claim to be without sin, we deceive ourselves and the truth is not in us. If we confess our sins, **he is faithful and just and will forgive us our sins and purify us from all unrighteousness.** If we claim we have not sinned, we make him out to be a liar and his word has no place in our lives. 1 John 1:8-10(NIV)

In addition, God's heart goes out to the one who was cheated as a very young child of a normal loving relationship with his father. He goes after the "little ones" and leads them back to himself. And we are instructed not to look down on them.

"See that you do not look down on one of these **little ones**. For I tell you that their angels in heaven always see the face of my Father in heaven.

"What do you think? If a man owns a hundred sheep, and one of them wanders away, will he not leave the ninety-nine on the hills and go to look for the one that wandered off? And if he finds it, I tell you the truth, he is happier about that one sheep than about the ninety-nine that did not wander off. In the same way your Father in heaven is not willing that any of these **little ones** should be lost. Matthew 18:10-14 (NIV)

Heterosexuals tend to make homosexuality the greatest of sins, but heterosexual sins are just as serious. Practicing homosexuals will not inherit the Kingdom of God, but neither will adulterers, the sexually immoral, male prostitutes, or those who practice any other sexual sin. Sexual sinners of any kind will not inherit the Kingdom, and neither will thieves, the greedy, drunkards, slanderers and swindlers.

Do you not know that **the wicked** will not inherit the kingdom of God? Do not be deceived: Neither the **sexually immoral** nor **idolaters** nor **adulterers** nor **male prostitutes** nor **homosexual offenders** nor **thieves** nor **the greedy** nor **drunkards** nor **slanderers** nor **swindlers** will inherit the kingdom of God. And **that is what some of you were. But you were washed, you were sanctified, you were justified in the name of the Lord Jesus Christ and by the Spirit of our God**. 1 Corinthians 6:9-11(NIV)

It is equally important to understand from these verses that it is possible to be cleansed and delivered from these sexual practices and sinful behaviors through the Lord Jesus Christ.

It is also very important to make a distinction between having sinful sexual temptations—homosexual or heterosexual—and giving in to these temptations and practicing them. Temptation is not sin. If you are tempted to have an adulterous affair, but you resist, you have not sinned. If you are tempted to have a homosexual relationship, but you resist, you have not sinned. Homosexuals and heterosexuals have the same challenge when it comes to resisting the temptation to sexually sin. Remember, Jesus was "tempted in every way, just as we are—yet was without sin." Hebrews 4:15(NIV) It says that he can "sympathize with our weaknesses" because he knows what it is like to be tempted.

The above verses do not say that homosexuals will not inherit the kingdom of God, but "homosexual offenders". Several other Bible translations (ESV, NET, HCSB, NLT) use the phrase "practice

108

homosexuality". If you have homosexual temptations, but you do not give into them, <u>you have not sinned</u>. You are not practicing homosexuality.

Also, recognize that you can be delivered from such sin. The same verses say "that is what some of you were". In other words, there were people in Corinth who practiced all of these sexual sins, and were labeled as such. But they were delivered and were no longer classified in these sinful categories.

Jesus knows that our perverted temptations are like a sickness inside of us. We need a doctor—a good doctor. Jesus is that great physician of our souls. He desires to make us whole again.

"It is not the healthy who need a doctor, but the sick. I have not come to call the righteous, but sinners to repentance." Luke 5:31-32(NIV)

He himself bore our sins in his body on the tree, so that we might die to sins and live for righteousness; **by his wounds you have been healed**. 1 Peter 2:24(NIV)

Becoming a Friend of Homosexuals

It would be a gross error to assume that all who have homosexual desires are pleased to have these desires and do not want to become heterosexual. Imagine for the moment that you found yourself as a teenager or young adult having homosexual desires and feeling bad about yourself and wanting to change. Where would you go for help? The active gay community would tell you that you were born that way and there is nothing you can do about it. And, they would encourage you to go ahead and practice what you feel. And the Christian community is primarily viewed as those who reject homosexuality and homosexuals (practicing or non-practicing). That leaves you all alone with no one to turn to for help.

What would Jesus do if a homosexual came to him wanting help? We know that Jesus came for sinners. Look again at Luke 5:31-32 above. He was a friend of sinners, and the theologians of the time mocked him for it. (Matthew 9:10-13, 11:19, Luke 5:30-32) If homosexuals are rejected by Christians, who else can they go to for support? How else are they to discover that Jesus came to manifest his character, purposes and will in our lives by the power of his Spirit within us and by his word? "For God is working in you, giving you the desire and the power to do what pleases him." Philippians 2:13 (NLT) How are they to have the desire to change or the power to do so if no one is there to lead them into the truth? How are they to know the love of God if we are not there to reveal his love through our love and acceptance?

Jesus is mankind's answer for all sin. Jesus did not come condemning us; he came to save us.

For the Son of Man came to seek and to save what was lost. Luke 19:10 (NIV)

But go and learn what this means: 'I desire mercy, not sacrifice.' For I have not come to call the righteous, but sinners. Matthew 9:13 (NIV)

If we, as Christians, do not come alongside of them and lead them to Jesus, who will? Rejecting them because they are homosexuals does not lead them to Jesus. In fact, it gives them the message that Jesus does not love them. Remember, we were all sinners to whom Jesus died while we were still sinners. (Romans 5:8)

And remember, a homosexual who chooses not to practice homosexuality has not sinned. But he needs others to come alongside of him to support him in his resolve to remain pure.

Also consider that homosexuals have an identity issue. They need masculine heterosexual men as friends as they work through their struggles with identity and any temptations. We are all in this struggle against sinful temptations of the flesh. We all need one another for support, encouragement, wise counsel and accountability. Why would we reject a homosexual over any other type of sin in someone's life?

Accept one another, then, just as Christ accepted you, **in order to bring praise to God**. Romans 15:7 (NIV)

Reflection questions

If you are struggling with homosexual temptations, how might your sexual identity have been misguided as a young boy?

Where do you need healing in this area of sexual identity or sexual sins?

How should we minister to anyone struggling with their own homosexual temptations? How do we love him?

Homosexuals need loving, masculine heterosexual role models for friends. Are you willing to be a friend to a homosexual? How are you struggling to love and accept them? (Matthew 7:1-5, Luke 18:9-14)

Chapter Fourteen

Reforming Sexual Identity through Jesus and our Heavenly Father

Our sexual identity may have become distorted by a number of influences. We may have had unloving fathers. We may have been sexually abused by a close relative—a father, mother, sister, brother, uncle or anyone close and presumably one to trust. We may not have been welcomed as a male by our father and brothers, and so we have never left the identity with our mother from birth. We may have had a controlling and domineering mother and a weak and passive father, which left us confused and misdirected sexually. We may have gotten into pornography, which now has a tight addictive grip on us. We may have become slaves of fornication and adultery.

How we see ourselves is very much tied to how we see ourselves sexually. Our sexual identity is not our entire identity, but it can dominate our attitudes and behavior. We need to seek out God's word and our heavenly Father in order to transform our thinking and attitudes about ourselves. We can be in a prison whose bars are misconceptions and lies about ourselves. They can hold us captive for our entire lives.

Jesus said, "**If you hold to my teaching**, you are really my disciples. Then you will know the truth, and **the truth will set you free**." John 8:31-32(NIV)

If we want to be free, we need to know the truth about God and about ourselves. In order to know this truth, we need to seek out the truth and allow it to transform our thinking by being obedient to what we learn.

Do not conform any longer to the pattern of this world, but **be transformed by the renewing of your mind**. Then you will be able to test and approve what God's will is—his good, pleasing and perfect will. Romans 12:2(NIV)

What Are True Man and Woman?

What is a man? Our culture lies to us—to both men and woman. Remember, the devil controls our culture. He lies to us through television, fads and fashions, magazines and the internet. He even lies to us through some of our churches and leaders.

What is the devil telling us? To the woman, he tells her that to be a real woman she needs to be beautiful with a sexy body. Little girls play with Barbie Dolls and from an early age see these perfect bodily figures—little sex objects—as their understanding of what a real woman looks like. Every woman's magazine supports this dream that is only true for about 1% of woman. And even for this 1%, the beauty fades away as the years pass by. The entire movie industry propagates the same image for woman. And now, with pornography, we take that 1%, strip her down stark naked, take photographs and videos of her exposing all her sexual parts, and then make these photos and videos available to lustful men around the world. Meanwhile, the other 99% have to compete against these exposed bodily beauties in order to captivate their husbands' and boyfriends' sexual attention. Both men and woman have been taken captive by the lie.

A woman's outward beauty is a beautiful part of God's creation that is given to please the eyes and touch of her husband, not the world. More importantly, her beauty goes far deeper than the outward appearance, which is fleeting with age. Her true beauty lies deep within her. She is much more than a body. She has a personality, and she has a spirit within her. What do they look like? What does the Bible say?

> Charm is deceptive, and beauty is fleeting; but a woman who fears the LORD is to be praised. Proverbs 31:30(NIV) (Take a look at Proverbs 31:10-31.)

> Your beauty should not come from outward adornment, such as braided hair and the wearing of gold jewelry and fine clothes. **Instead, it should be that of your inner self, the unfading beauty of a gentle and quiet spirit, which is of great worth in God's sight.** For this is the way the holy women of the past **who put their hope in God used to make themselves beautiful.** 1 Peter 3:3-5(NIV)

We see from just these few verses that a woman's lasting and most valuable beauty is not her outward appearance, but her inward character that comes from knowing God. That is how women should see themselves. That is how men should look at women! Instead of lusting after her beautiful body, we should be looking for the character of God that lives within her.

Now, what about man? How has man been defined by the devil's culture? Man has been lied to just as much, if not more than women. How has man been portrayed? Look at the truck sales in this country. Companies like Ford, have made more money on truck sales than other models. Why is that? Do we have a lot of construction workers and farmers in this country? Do men do a lot of hauling that requires a truck? Most of the trucks I see are driven by men who rarely use the bed that rides behind them. What is our culture telling men? Trucks make a real man! A real man

114

is rugged and strong! Skinny and weak men are wimps! Football players are real men! Tough and mean! Real men are handsome and in control. Good athletes are real men. Real men have great careers and make lots of money. Real men are smart and have all the answers. They are confident and bold. Just like a woman's outward beauty, the world's view of a real man is mostly physical dimensions, adornments and outward appeal. We can be wimps inside, but outwardly we want to appear strong, powerful and handsome.

But how does God define a real man?

This is what the LORD says: "Let not the wise man boast of his **wisdom** or the strong man boast of his **strength** or the rich man boast of his **riches**, but let him who boasts boast about this: that he **understands and knows me, that I am the LORD, who exercises kindness, justice and righteousness on earth, for in these I delight,**" declares the LORD. Jeremiah 9:23-24(NIV)

The inner man is what counts. God knows the inner man, and it is the inner man that God transforms. The outer man is wasting away, but the inner man is being transformed day by day through the Spirit of God within us.

Therefore we do not lose heart. Though **outwardly we are wasting away**, yet **inwardly we are being renewed day by day**. 2 Corinthians 4:16 (NIV)

And we, who with unveiled faces all reflect the Lord's glory, **are being transformed into his likeness with ever-increasing glory**, which comes from the Lord, who is the Spirit. 2 Corinthians 3:18(NIV)

This is the essence of becoming a real man, being transformed into the likeness of Jesus.

Dear friends, now we are children of God, and what we will be has not yet been made known. But we know that **when he appears, we shall be like him, for we shall see him as he is**. Everyone who has this hope in him purifies himself, just as he is pure. 1 John 3:2-3(NIV)

Identity with Jesus

Jesus is a real man! If we want to be real men, we need to model our lives after his. We need to reject the identity given to us from our youth and take on our true identity in Christ Jesus, the only true man. He is the man to model. He is both Son of God and Son of Man. We are to receive his Spirit and become like him, the real man.

Jesus was not influenced by peer pressure. He did not conform to the culture in order to be accepted. He did not fall to the temptations of his flesh nor the devil. When his heavenly Father called him to minister, God placed his Holy Spirit upon him and the Spirit led him out into the desert to fast for forty days and to be tempted by the devil.

Then Jesus was led by the Spirit into the desert to be tempted by the devil. After fasting forty days and forty nights, he was hungry. The tempter came to him and said, "If you are the Son of God, tell these stones to become bread." Matthew 4:1-3(NIV)

A real man has control over his fleshly desires. Jesus commanded his body to go without food for forty days. And when tempted by the devil to turn the stones into bread, he refused, even though his body was at the point of death from a lack of food for nearly six weeks. A real man stands up against temptation and does what is right in the eyes of God. It does not matter how many muscles he has, how great an athlete he may be. He doesn't have to be wealthy or own a big truck. He just needs to know God, know what is right, and then be in control of himself so he can do what is right. Jesus was a real man, and that is what he did.

Jesus was rejected by men for who he was. They ridiculed him, slandered him, spit upon him, lied about him and falsely accused him. They tortured him and hung him upon a cross and killed him. At any time he could have called down ten thousand angels to wipe out his attackers, but he did not. Only a real man could withstand the load that he carried.

Then Jesus went with his disciples to a place called Gethsemane, and he said to them, "Sit here while I go over there and pray." He took Peter and the two sons of Zebedee along with him, and he **began to be sorrowful and troubled**. Then he said to them, "**My soul is overwhelmed with sorrow to the point of death**. Stay here and keep watch with me."

Going a little farther, **he fell with his face to the ground and prayed, "My Father, if it is possible, may this cup be taken from me. Yet not as I will, but as you will**." Matthew 26:36-39(NIV)

An angel from heaven appeared to him and strengthened him. And **being in anguish, he prayed more earnestly, and his sweat was like drops of blood falling to the ground.** Luke 22:43-44(NIV)

When the soldiers came to take him captive, he did not give in to fear. He could have called down angels from heaven to rescue him, but he resolved to do his Father's will. Real men obey God.

"Put your sword back in its place," Jesus said to him, "for all who draw the sword will die by the sword. **Do you think I cannot call on my Father, and he will at once put at my disposal more than twelve legions of angels?** But how then would the Scriptures be fulfilled that say it must happen in this way?" Matthew 26:52-54(NIV)

As his enemies took his life on a torturous cross, he asked for his Father to forgive them.

Two other men, both criminals, were also led out with him to be executed. When they came to the place called the Skull, there they crucified him, along with the criminals—one on his right, the other on his left. Jesus said, "**Father, forgive them, for they do not know what they are doing.**" Luke 23:32-34(NIV)

Real men forgive and seek restoration for their offenders. Real men know God and live their lives in obedience to God. Others can see God through the actions and character of real men. Real men can stand alone in a crowd, knowing that their identity is not among men, but that true identity is in God

Identity with our Heavenly Father

God is the one with true masculine beauty. His beauty is beyond comprehension. The sight of his beauty will bring pleasure for eternity because his beauty is infinite.

One thing I ask of the LORD, this is what I seek: that I may dwell in the house of the LORD all the days of my life, to **gaze upon the beauty of the LORD and to seek him** in his temple. Psalm 27:4(NIV)

We need to see our heavenly Father in order to see God's intent for manliness. Satan drives to pervert fathers so that their sons and daughters will not perceive their heavenly Father as a father of love and wisdom and strength. This is true beauty, and it comes from the Lord. If we want to become real men, we need to seek out our heavenly Father, to submit to him and trust him as one who loves us and desires good things for us. He promises to give us his own Spirit to live within us.

"So I say to you: Ask and it will be given to you; seek and you will find; knock and the door will be opened to you. For everyone who asks receives; he who seeks finds; and to him who knocks, the door will be opened.

"Which of you fathers, if your son asks for a fish, will give him a snake instead? Or if he asks for an egg, will give him a scorpion? If you then, though you are evil, know how to give good gifts to your children, **how much more will your Father in heaven give the Holy Spirit to those who ask him!**" Luke 11:9-13(NIV)

Our heavenly Father is pleased to give us his kingdom. He gives us all things, the things of this life and the things of his kingdom. Seeking his kingdom and his character is becoming a real man.

Do not be afraid, little flock, for your Father has been pleased to give you the kingdom. Luke 12:32(NIV)

So do not worry, saying, 'What shall we eat?' or 'What shall we drink?' or 'What shall we wear?' For the pagans run after all these things, and your heavenly Father knows that you need them. **But seek first his kingdom and his righteousness**, and all these things will be given to you as well. Therefore do not worry about tomorrow, for tomorrow will worry about itself. Each day has enough trouble of its own. Matthew 6:31-34(NIV)

Jesus taught us to pray,

"This, then, is how you should pray: "'Our Father in heaven, hallowed be your name, **your kingdom come, your will be done on earth as it is in heaven.** Matthew 6:9-10

Real men fight for his kingdom to come. This is not a battle fought with guns, fists and knives. It is a battle fought with the truth of God. It is a battle fought with righteous living so that others can see God through us. It is a battle of prayer so that God's will is "done on earth as it is in heaven". It is a battle of loving God and our fellow man, rather than cursing God and offending those around us. This is not a battle for wimps. It is a battle for real men, men of God who live for God and become like him.

From the days of John the Baptist until now, the kingdom of heaven has been forcefully advancing, and **forceful men lay hold of it**. Matthew 11:12(NIV)

God desires for us to become real men, like his Son Jesus. As a loving father, he instructs us and disciplines us for our own good so that we can share in his holiness and become men of God.

In your struggle against sin, you have not yet resisted to the point of shedding your blood. And you have forgotten that word of encouragement that addresses you as sons: "My son, do not make light of the Lord's discipline, and do not lose heart when he rebukes you, because the Lord disciplines those he loves, and he punishes everyone he accepts as a son."

Endure hardship as discipline; God is treating you as sons. For what son is not disciplined by his father? If you are not disciplined (and everyone undergoes discipline), then you are illegitimate children and not true sons. Moreover, we have all had human fathers who disciplined us and we respected them for it. How much more should we submit to the Father of our spirits and live! Our fathers disciplined us for a little while as they thought best; but God disciplines us for our good, that we may share in his holiness. No discipline seems pleasant at the time, but painful. Later on, however, it produces a harvest of righteousness and peace for those who have been trained by it. Hebrews 12:4-11(NIV)

Identity struggles are simple, but difficult. We do not make the transformation into the image of God overnight just because we desire it. The transformation is a continual process that is wrought out in time by a cooperative and obedient relationship with God by his indwelling Holy Spirit. Our struggles can be many, such as the struggle with our sexual identity, our addictions to pornography, our view of a real man or our view of the true beauty of a woman. We also have to get past all of the wounds inflicted upon us from the time we were just infants, many of which may be hidden from us. Transformation for anyone is a lifetime process that requires faith in God and obedient perseverance.

Jesus came to make us victorious. He came to transform our lowly nature into his holy nature, and he will accomplish this in time if we persevere over time. There will be struggles and pain, but this is part of the transformation.

I consider that our **present sufferings** are not worth comparing with the glory that will be revealed in us. The creation **waits** in eager expectation for the sons of God to be revealed. For the **creation was subjected to frustration, not by its own choice, but by the will of the one who subjected it, in hope that the creation itself will be liberated from its bondage to decay and brought into the glorious freedom of the children of God**.

We know that the whole creation has been groaning as in the pains of childbirth right up to the present time. Not only so, but we ourselves, who have the firstfruits of the Spirit, groan inwardly as we wait eagerly for our adoption as sons, the redemption of our bodies. **For in this hope we were saved**. But hope that is seen is no hope at all. Who hopes for what he already has? But if we hope for what we do not yet have, we **wait for it patiently**. Romans 8:18-25(NIV)

Even though this transformation is lengthy and sometimes frustrating and painful, we are not doing this in our own strength. Jesus sent his Spirit to live within us. He is the one who is working within us to bring about the likeness of Jesus in our character and identity.

Now the Lord is the Spirit, and where the Spirit of the Lord is, there is freedom. And we, who with unveiled faces all reflect the Lord's glory, are **being transformed into his likeness with ever-increasing glory, which comes from the Lord, who is the Spirit**. 2 Corinthians 3:17-18(NIV)

Perseverance is difficult because it requires for us to struggle for a long time. In the case of our identity, it will take years. In fact, the process will not be complete until we see Jesus face to face. For a homosexual to have his identity transformed into a functioning heterosexual, the transformation will take years. A sex addict will struggle against sin for his lifetime, as everyone struggles against sin throughout our lives. The key is that we should rapidly become victorious as we give our life and will over to Jesus Christ. We are instructed not to become weary and not to give up.

Let us **not become weary** in doing good, for at the proper time we will reap a harvest **if we do not give up**. Galatians 6:9(NIV)

Neither are we to become discouraged. The struggle, the hardship and the pain are all indications that something is being transformed within us. It is a sign that we are fighting the good fight against our sinful nature. This is a good thing. We need to count on Jesus to take us through.

Consider it pure joy, my brothers, whenever you face trials of many kinds, because you know that the testing of your faith develops perseverance. **Perseverance must finish its work so that you may be mature and complete, not lacking anything**. James 1:2-4(NIV)

...being confident of this, that **he who began a good work in you will carry it on to completion until the day of Christ Jesus**. Philippians 1:6(NIV)

In this world there will be trials and temptations. Our hope is in the day when Jesus returns; then the battle will be over. We will be transformed in an instant. As we struggle, it is this hope that God sees in us and keeps us pure in his sight. (1 John 3:1-3, 1 Corinthians 15:51-54). The key is to "fight the good fight". In time, we will have the victory.

But you, man of God, **flee from all this, and pursue righteousness, godliness, faith, love, endurance and gentleness. Fight the good fight of the faith. Take hold of the eternal life to which you were called** when you made your good confession in the presence of many witnesses. 1 Timothy 6:11-12(NIV)

Reflection questions

How can you seek out the true beauty of women?

How do you view your own masculinity?

How do you think God sees you as a man?

In what way is God calling you to become a real man?

How are you persevering in your fight against your old identity? Where do you need to be encouraged?

Chapter Fifteen

Our Marriage with God

God created marriage, and he created our sexual union as part of that marriage. Our marriages are only for this earthly existence. Jesus told us that there will be no marriages or married men or women after we are raised from the dead. (Matthew 22:23-30) Even though our marriages are only temporary, lasting only for our lifetime, they have a powerful significance. Our marriages were created by God to give us a picture and a testimony of our eternal marriage to Jesus Christ. He is the true man and the lasting husband.

Jesus' Marriage with His People Is First

God has given us earthly marriages between a man and woman as a living picture of the marriage of Jesus with his Bride, the Church. As we look at the following passage about marriage, look at how Paul is making a repetitive comparison of our earthly marriage to the marriage of Christ to his Church. Our relationships between husbands and wives are a mirror of our relationship with Christ and his relationship with us.

> Wives, submit to your own husbands, as to the Lord. For the husband is the head of the wife even **as Christ is the head of the**

church, his body, and is himself its Savior. Now **as the church submits to Christ**, so also wives should submit in everything to their husbands.

Husbands, love your wives, **as Christ loved the church** and gave himself up for her, that he might sanctify her, having cleansed her by the washing of water with the word, so that he might present the church to himself in splendor, without spot or wrinkle or any such thing, that she might be holy and without blemish. In the same way husbands should love their wives as their own bodies. He who loves his wife loves himself. For no one ever hated his own flesh, but nourishes and cherishes it, **just as Christ does the church**, because we are members of his body. "Therefore a man shall leave his father and mother and hold fast to his wife, and the two shall become one flesh." **This mystery is profound, and I am saying that it refers to Christ and the church**. However, let each one of you love his wife as himself, and let the wife see that she respects her husband. Ephesians 5:22-33(ESV)

Jesus compares his second coming with a bridegroom coming for his bride (Matthew 25:1-13). John's Revelation reveals more details of this marriage.

Then I heard what sounded like a great multitude, like the roar of rushing waters and like loud peals of thunder, shouting:
"Hallelujah!
For our Lord God Almighty reigns.
Let us rejoice and be glad
and give him glory!
For the wedding of the Lamb has come,
and his bride has made herself ready.
Fine linen, bright and clean,
was given her to wear."
(Fine linen stands for the righteous acts of the saints.)

125

Then the angel said to me, "Write: 'Blessed are those who are invited **to the wedding supper of the Lamb**!'" And he added, "These are the true words of God." Revelation 19:6-9

Notice in the next passage how we, his bride, are described as the living city of the new Jerusalem. This is a place where God will dwell for eternity. (Read Ephesians 2:19-22 & 1 Peter 2:4-5)

Then I saw a new heaven and a new earth, for the first heaven and the first earth had passed away, and there was no longer any sea. I saw the Holy City, the new Jerusalem, coming down out of heaven from God, prepared **as a bride beautifully dressed for her husband**. And I heard a loud voice from the throne saying, "Now the dwelling of God is with men, and he will live with them. They will be his people, and God himself will be with them and be their God. Revelation 21:1-3(NIV)

One of the seven angels who had the seven bowls full of the seven last plagues came and said to me, "Come, I will show you **the bride, the wife of the Lamb**." Revelation 21:9(NIV)

Old Testament Marriage with God

God has always seen his people as his bride. Unfortunately, his people have always pursued other lovers and aroused the intense jealousy of God. The Ten Commandments bear this out.

"You shall have no other gods before me.
"You shall not make for yourself an idol in the form of anything in heaven above or on the earth beneath or in the waters below. You shall not bow down to them or worship them; for **I, the Lord your God,**

am a jealous God, punishing the children for the sin of the fathers to the third and fourth generation of those who hate me, Exodus 20:3-5(NIV)

Do not worship any other god, for the LORD, **whose name is Jealous, is a jealous God**. Exodus 34:14(NIV)

In spite of God's warning and commands, they went after the gods of all the nations around them, even enemy nations. They took on their practices, worshipped their gods and sought out their favor and blessings— while they ignored the promises of the one true lover who could truly bless them. God, their husband, accuses them of adultery and prostitution.

"Why should I forgive you? Your children have forsaken me and sworn by gods that are not gods. I supplied all their needs, yet **they committed adultery and thronged to the houses of prostitutes**. They are well-fed, lusty stallions, **each neighing for another man's wife**. Should I not punish them for this?" declares the LORD. "Should I not avenge myself on such a nation as this? Jeremiah 5:7-9(NIV)

This is your lot, the portion I have decreed for you," declares the LORD, "because you have forgotten me and trusted in false gods. I will pull up your skirts over your face that your shame may be seen—**your adulteries and lustful neighings, your shameless prostitution!** I have seen your detestable acts on the hills and in the fields. Woe to you, O Jerusalem! How long will you be unclean?" Jeremiah 13:25-27(NIV)

There are many other references to this point, such as Ezekiel 16:23-43 & 23:1-30. It should be noticed that God sees our relationship with him as a marriage. He also makes it very clear that our marriage with him is to be sexually pure. In other words, we are not to engage in intimate or worshipful relationships with anything in this life that would replace God as our loving Lord, master, provider, protector and identity. To do so would be to commit adultery or prostitution.

Even though our earthly marriages are temporary, we should keep them sexually pure in honor of God. First, we honor him because he created marriage to be pure. Secondly, we honor him in marriage in order to honor our eternal marriage with Christ. Throughout history, the fall of a nation can be seen when marriage and the sexual union between husband and wife is no longer honored. Nations fall when there is divorce, adultery, prostitution, homosexuality, and sexual impurity of any kind. We cannot fool God. We will reap what we sow. He created marriage to be sexually honored. It comes down to our choices.

The Devil Is Intent to Pollute and Pervert the Divine Image of Marriage

It should be no wonder that sex is the issue and craze of our generation and generations of the past. Premarital sex (fornication), adultery, prostitution, divorce, unmarried living together, children born out of wedlock, homosexuality, pornography, rape, sexual abuse, lust, promiscuity, sexual profanity, sex throughout family members other than husband and wife, sexual humor, sexual entertainment, and any other sexual deviation from God's original intent. All of these are part of our culture. Most are accepted and in many places lifted up. We are destroying ourselves without understanding.

Our guilt is inexcusable, but we have one who is intent on destroying the picture of God's marriage to his bride. The devil was called the "prince of this world" by Jesus (John 12:31, 14:30 & 16:11). He has a master plan to rob us of our life with Christ, to kill and destroy.

The thief *(devil)* comes only to steal and kill and destroy; I *(Jesus)* have come that they may have life, and have it to the full. John 10:10(NIV) (Italics added for clarity.)

If the devil can pervert and destroy the family, he can pervert and destroy the Church. The Church is not an organization that thrives on buildings, programs, organizations and staff. The Church is the living body of our Lord Jesus Christ. The life of his body is borne out in our daily lives. The central focus of our lives comes back to families. Without solid families our nation will fall. In fact, we are seeing the evidence of this corruption today in this nation. Many seeds of destruction have been planted within the family, but most of them revolve around how we perceive and practice sex. If we want the life that Jesus promises those who seek him, we must repent of our sinful sexual practices and uphold sex within a marriage as sacred and created for life. Not just biological life, but life eternal. We cannot separate our sexual practices and attitudes from our relationship with God.

Reflection questions

How have you made God jealous? What are your idols? How have you turned away from his love for you?

How have you defamed your marriage to God by defaming earthly marriage and the role of sex in marriage? How have you honored God with your marriage and sexual purity?

How has the devil deceived you and used you to distort and pervert the view of the sexual union between a married man and woman?

How have you dishonored God with your sexual impurity?

How do you honor your marriage with Jesus by your submission to him in all aspects and places of your life?

Eternal life starts with the day you repent of your old life and pursue a new life in Jesus. (Matthew 7:13-14, Luke 9:23-27) How have you repented? How have you given up your life in this world in order to pursue eternal life? Describe your new life in comparison to your old life.

60568263R00077

Made in the USA
Lexington, KY
10 February 2017